IS YOUR GLASS HALF EMPTY?

Lessons for Project Managers and
Their Managers from Thirty Years in the
Project Business

JAMES ROY

authorHOUSE®

AuthorHouse™
1663 Liberty Drive
Bloomington, IN 47403
www.authorhouse.com
Phone: 1-800-839-8640

First published by AuthorHouse   5/24/2011

ISBN: 978-1-4567-6541-5 (e)
ISBN: 978-1-4567-6542-2 (dj)
ISBN: 978-1-4567-6543-9 (sc)

Library of Congress Control Number: 2011907416

Printed in the United States of America

ACKNOWLEDGMENTS

(And My First Piece of Advice)

I would like to acknowledge my wife, for her contributions to this book. Throughout my business career, with very long hours and seemingly continuous travel, she was usually very patient, was always supportive, and did an outstanding job of raising our three well-educated children, who are now very fine citizens. Her support was not always properly acknowledged, but it allowed me to continue following my passion.

Thanks to her for allowing me to first learn what I did about the business so that I could present it here, hopefully for the benefit of others.

The first lesson, therefore, is that if you have a passion for project work and follow my advice about traveling to project sites, you need a partner who is willing to live with your extensive travel.

CONTENTS

Is Your Glass Half Empty or Half Full? Can You Tolerate Detail? Can You
Be Honest, Open and Transparent with Good and Bad News? Are You Free
to Travel Away from the Office? Are You Comfortable with Confrontation
When It Is Necessary? Are You a Team Player? Can You Take an Interest
in the Accounting Side?

Plan and Manage the Variances: Plan Number 1 The Scope Definition and
Plans: Plan Number 2 The Schedule Plan: Plan Number 3 The Cost Plan:
Cost Risks and Opportunities and Cost Variance Tracking: Plan Number
4 The Earned Progress Plan: Quantity Progress Curves: Managing
Variances including Schedule Variances: Cost Variances and Earned
Progress Variances: Productivity and Management of Contingencies.

Administration in General: The Contract with Your Customer

Contractors in General: The Contract Is Critical: How Much Oversight is
appropriate? Contract Default and Termination.

PREFACE

Managing the intricacies of multitask projects can be fraught with peril, as both customer satisfaction and project profitability hang in the balance. The difference between success and failure in such ventures ultimately rests in the hands of the project manager. Over the years, I've seen remarkable project managers save otherwise doomed projects, and conversely, I've seen how poor project management practices can scuttle potentially successful projects.

Over a long career in managing projects, I've compiled my own list of best practices in managing projects; I've also learned what makes an effective manager of project managers. I've captured these observations here in an attempt to share them with others who are, or could be, project managers or who are responsible for managing multiple project managers in a project-based business.

My objective is to define what I see as the critical traits and philosophies held by project managers and to highlight the mistakes made by project managers and their management. In each case, I will show what should be the routine practices of a successful project manager or project business manager.

All of this is based on over three decades of managing projects and managers of projects. I'll use many anecdotes from my own experience as illustrations. I'll also share my experience working under a variety of general managers and show how their behavior, both good and bad, impacted the various projects under their control.

What you will *not* find here is a complete how-to guide to project management, such as learning how to input logic into a computer-based system, how to maintain a program like Primavera, how to create a Work Breakdown Structure, how to maintain an operating statement, how to write the details of contract terms and conditions, or how to turn over a contract to the customer. This information and many more necessary processes can be readily found in a variety of other texts and videos.

Over the years, I have formed some very basic ideas about project management. Most of these ideas concern the many traits, processes, practices, and philosophies that are critical to consistent success in the project business. Admittedly, my ideas are considered by many to be quite controversial. I believe that this can be understood after reading about my background and the mentors who have influenced my career.

As an example, one of my fundamental concepts is that successful project managers typically view the world as a glass that is always half empty, a pessimist if you will; they believe in Murphy's Law: "Whatever can go wrong, will" (and you better have a contingency plan).

Another concept is the importance of confronting the variances to a detailed plan in an open and honest way, both with oneself and with others. This, of course, means that there must be a plan for schedule and for cost in the first place. I do not subscribe to what someone once told me: "Real men [or women] do not use the critical path method."

I am comfortable writing in the first person and might be guilty of being a little repetitious. I have always believed in the wisdom of telling you what I'm going to say, saying it, and finally telling you what I said.

The Author's Background

Before I ask you to buy into these concepts, it will be helpful to briefly review my background in business and project management. This will allow you to judge the value of what I say.

I began my career working in an operational position for a major corporation. Like many of my peers at the time, I planned to be there for life. Once I had the opportunity to assess my work environment, I realized that people were assigned as "project managers" if they had failed elsewhere. In my early experience, project management was kind of the "penalty box" in many businesses.

Naturally, I avoided any project management "opportunity" and progressed well until a change in government contracts put me in a project management position. I was responsible for building a prototype of a naval nuclear submarine propulsion system, valued at several hundred million dollars, in New York State.

The assignment, to build a demonstration and training facility, was probably over my head at that time, but I decided it was an opportunity to learn, and I was determined to make it work. Eight years later, after successfully completing the project (probably a surprise to many, including myself), I was rewarded with a substantial operational position, one sought by many. But I had been bitten by the project management bug. I was completely caught up in the exhilaration of starting with an idea and then coordinating the many engineering, procurement, and building skills required to successfully complete a valuable project. I had a difficult time walking away, both mentally and physically, from this, my first real project.

My new operational position dealt with ongoing production and maintenance, with an emphasis on continuing improvements in cost and quality. Compared to life as a project manager, it soon became boring and certainly did not get my full attention.

After two and one half years, I moved to the commercial project business in the same company, taking with me the discipline I had learned in the naval nuclear business and the project management lessons from the long submarine demonstration project. I was delighted.

I was fortunate to land a position managing a group doing turnkey installations of small electric power generating stations internationally. I had never used a passport for anything but trips to Canada and the Caribbean and knew nothing of commercial balance sheets and operating statements. On my naval project, the government was only worried about the projected extent of overruns so that the proper account or appropriation could be charged. So here I was in the commercial world, learning a whole new discipline.

One of the more exhilarating things that happened in my new assignment was being called back from a delightful vacation trip to the Caribbean to lead an evaluation of a large international power project, which was in deep overrun; and where the company was about to sign a contract for an extension. I knew it! Suddenly I was asked to assume the project management role. Over the next four years, I made over sixty trips to the Middle East, managing this and other projects. This is where I gained my first experience managing other project managers.

When the market for power generation equipment declined, our company consolidated groups in the project business from various equipment businesses. I somehow "survived" and was named manager of projects of the consolidated group, and I began spending a lot of time in some of the most unpleasant places on this earth.

Faced with a protracted decline in the traditional power generation market, the business turned to alternate fuel projects, including using refuse-derived fuel (garbage), whole tires, wood chips, and even agricultural waste as fuel for new power stations all over this country. These were unique, one-of-a-kind configurations that presented a whole host of challenges to designers and builders alike.

I recognized that the company was growing more disenchanted with the increased risk and lower margins of these projects, so after twenty-seven years with the company, I sought greener pastures, accepting a position to manage the Power Division of an international architect engineering firm that had reportedly landed several large turnkey projects.

I must admit that I had performed very poor due diligence in my selection of a new employer, and I left within a year, wondering why I had believed their story of the expected large turnkey projects.

At a second architect engineering company, I began in a special projects role and soon earned control of all the project activities. This was a small company where I had to find and win contracts for my own business. After the company was acquired by a larger firm, I ended up as a Senior VP for Business Development for both our company and another architect engineering company serving the industrial and power generation arenas.

On paper it was a fine position, but I realized I was no longer having fun. I missed managing projects and decided to return to a large power equipment supplier, a competitor to my first company in the business of large projects. I was soon directing the organization responsible for the delivery of all equipment and for execution of turnkey construction projects, a position similar to what I had left at my first company.

Suddenly, the domestic US power generation market exploded in a very positive way; I needed to hire and train project managers and reorganize in order to manage a fivefold increase in the number of projects. Almost overnight, we had one hundred active domestic and international projects. This learning curve was as steep as the one I climbed twenty years earlier when I came to a commercial business from government contracting.

Because the companies in that business were overselling the technology in the equipment, I spent the next several years negotiating equipment non-performance-related settlements with subcontractors, partners, and customers. This was fun, and there were many lessons learned, particularly in the area of contract administration. It also inspired me to join the Neutral Panel with the American Arbitration Association after my retirement. The training was great, but I found that the legal community tried very hard to ensure that only attorneys sat on the arbitration panels.

I served as an expert witness on project management in several arbitration cases, which gave me further insight into just how poorly projects can be run and certainly validated, at least to myself, the convictions and positions that I will address in this book.

Looking back at my own career, I realized that I emulated or tapped into what I had learned either directly or indirectly from two larger-than-life figures, each of which had made substantial contributions to his chosen field. They were Admiral H. G. Rickover, father of the

American nuclear navy, and Jack Welch, former chairman and CEO of the General Electric Company.

Each of these men had a reputation for just plain "getting things done" and for being a "very tough boss." I am not sure about the getting things done part, but clearly I picked up enough of their traits to be considered a tough boss in my own right.

Admiral H. G. Rickover is widely recognized as the Father of the American nuclear navy. The man was solely responsible for what was probably the strongest deterrent and contributing factor to the end of the cold war: the stealth fleet of nuclear submarines around the world. This was made possible by nuclear propulsion, which allowed very extensive deployments under the ocean.

The "Admiral," as we knew him, had a most unique and effective information system, even before today's expansion in communications technology. He communicated personally, with direct contact with dozens and dozens of people in key positions.

As a young contractor manager of a nuclear reactor training facility, I was required to write him weekly reports outlining my critical issues or most critical problems. Routinely, my boss would be required to comment on my letter, and I would often hear back the next day from the Admiral. The feedback was not usually an "atta boy." Later as I took on more responsibility, I was given an opportunity, which I could not refuse, to call the Admiral weekly with basically the same type of message.

It took me awhile to figure out two of the Admiral's objectives in requiring these reports. First, he and his interested staff were kept informed on a timely basis, as was my boss. Even more important was what the letters and calls did for me. They forced me to prepare, to stop and think about what was important and where I should be spending my time.

Part of that thinking involved responding to the issues and creating contingency plans. I once told the Admiral that I was "on schedule," only to receive a long lecture about never referring to a schedule without detailing the schedule source, revision, and date of issue.

The value of this routine introspection was drummed into me, and I used it long after to gain valuable information and to train subordinates as well as project and field managers. I required these managers to identify their most critical issues in their regular communications and in structured monthly reports. Most of my teams figured out the two reasons for requiring it. Some did not, and some chose not to be entirely truthful or complete in their communications. These latter two groups soon left the world of project management, at least in my company.

Over time, I found that many project managers are very reluctant to be honest and candid about certain issues in their projects. In fact, I concluded that some do not want to even think about their most critical issues, let alone share them. I will comment later in different chapters on why I believe that so many project managers act this way. Because of this observation and what I had learned from others, my glass was almost always "half empty" when it came to relying exclusively on input from the project teams.

The Admiral supplemented his information flow by using a matrix organization, where senior functional people would be charged with monitoring the performance of projects or operations for which they were not fully responsible. Later in this text, I will describe a matrix organization where people are assigned to project teams from functional groups responsible for their training and performance. These functional leaders should be charged with tracking performance in their functional disciplines and disclosing issues that are unreported through the operating project team leadership.

Another element of the Admiral's information system was to simply "go look." He liked to just drop in unannounced; once upon a surprise arrival, he told me he was there to "sell Girl Scout cookies." I was unprepared and the subject of his wrath. Obviously I did not get a chance to buy any macaroons. His plan called for contractor executives and his staff, even those not directly responsible, to show up at all hours and distant locations to see what was really going on and make reports back to him and his staff.

This was the first series of true "reality shows." Edward Carlson, chief executive at United Airlines reinforced this message when I read his article. Carlson was responsible for turning the company around, at least for a while. His method was "management by walking around." He did more than walk. He traveled more than 200,000 miles a year in pursuit of "visible management." He wanted to meet employees and have them meet him, but the real value was in learning about how things were going around the company.

As a manager of projects, it was obvious to me that it was a must to schedule frequent reviews of each project with the entire team, using a format structured to touch on all important project elements, along with the manager's thoughts on critical issues. Certainly, as with my letters to the Admiral, cut-and-pasted content using old material was not acceptable. I demanded current thinking and a fresh look at all key project parameters.

Unfortunately, many of these techniques are not well accepted in our corporate cultures today. I recall meeting a project manager late one very snowy evening at an airport in the Midwest; after our meeting, I asked him to drive me to the construction site (about twenty miles away) for a surprise visit to the second shift. He expressed surprise and concern, because the second shift had not been "staged." I learned a lot that evening about our labor difficulties.

Needless to say, the Admiral promoted high standards of performance and was intolerant of sustained weak performers. He, like Jack Welch, removed such individuals, including executives. I found that in most cases, line managers knew those individuals were weak but they did not have the courage to take action. On the other hand, the Admiral would readily recognize a strong performance. Once I entered a meeting with him, expecting to have to go several rounds before my knockout, but he stunned me with "You are doing a good job, how are you doing it?" He laughed at my reaction; all I could do was stammer in surprise. On another occasion, I saw him berate an overweight colleague, eventually extracting a reluctant promise to lose weight. He could show tough love, a trait that he certainly demonstrated at that meeting.

Doing whatever had to be done to get results was another trait that he taught. He would readily approach the leaders of the government's executive and legislative branches or call top executives in any large corporation when he thought necessary. He was not slowed by either the chain of command or by the lines of management responsibilities.

One time, after inviting a chief executive of one of the largest US construction companies to a meeting, I saw him summarily excuse the executive, better yet throw the executive out, when they disagreed about performance standards. Certainly these management techniques are not good for all or even most situations, but there is value in having the courage to do whatever is necessary when "business as usual" does not solve the problem.

While I could go on, let me conclude my comments on the Admiral by noting his expectation for attention to detail. He told me once that project management was easy, it was nothing but "managing a list of lists." While this is simplified and misses the dimensions of time and cost, I found it to be a pretty good definition. I concluded that if you are not oriented to detail, there is no place for you in true project management.

I did not have the same direct relationship with Jack Welch but relied upon commentary from GE's management chain and the several books and business articles written about "America's Foremost CEO." Welch, former chairman and chief executive officer of General Electric, was a doer and strong leader. He may not like to be linked with a government figure, but like the Admiral, he was totally intolerant of poor performers; he recognized that a certain percentage of any unit would be poor performers and need to be replaced. He was right. He also had very high expectations for performance and achievement. From my distance, Jack also recognized that the company could not be run, and customers could not be satisfied, by sitting in his office.

As an executive, Jack was innovative. It seemed that he was routinely searching for new programs to implement in an effort to change the company's culture for the better. Unlike other companies that I have had experience with, these programs were not just the "fad of the year." This is a key lesson for managers of projects: set a course, a strategy, but never be afraid to make changes that you have thought through.

Jack also found a way to shrink GE's hierarchical structure; he could reach down through the layers in any organization to find out what was really going on.

I once fell into disfavor with senior management at a different company when I gave one of the managers a copy of one of Jack's books. I assume that the fact that the management was so weak by comparison that they took my action as a strong criticism.

So that is the background that shaped my career and influenced my approach to management. At my retirement event, a friend presented me with a burger box from McDonald's, signifying my encounters with poor or marginal performers that were often characterized as "Big Mac Attacks," playing off my name.

Yes, I had developed an understanding of what I wanted and how projects should be run, and I was openly intolerant of those who would not try to learn that approach. I was often harsh and autocratic with those individuals, until they came around or we agreed on their departure. Perhaps rationalizing, I thought of it as a form of that tough love. All of us have our limits, which vary with the environment. I certainly did and felt that there was no shame in reaching one's limits as long as a good effort had been made. I kept most of my friendships outside of my workplace.

You now know the specific project background that brings me to write this book. All of these concepts may not apply to all areas of project management, but I believe they apply to most, beginning with simple, single discipline (consulting, procurement, engineering, or construction) projects.

This book certainly does apply to large design and build projects, sometimes called EPC (engineer, procure, and construct) or turnkey projects, especially those bid on a conceptual design basis, and to the category of projects known in the industrial world as Lump Sum Turnkey (LSTK) projects. It applies to projects for the delivery of large equipment, particularly equipment with extensive support systems, systems that can be customer or location specific.

As I stated earlier, I have included sections on the key issues of interest to managers of project managers; I will devote sections to organization and staffing, managing large subcontractors, international projects, and extended scope projects. I will also address fast track projects, that is, projects where the phases of engineering or procurement or construction or startup/commissioning overlap each other for scheduler advantage.

This book can be helpful even if you feel your projects are too small. Most of the important traits and philosophies of a good project manager apply to projects of all sizes. You might even enjoy some of the anecdotes.

CHAPTER 1.

OVERVIEW OF PROJECT DEFINITIONS AND VARYING COMPLEXITIES

Before I dive into my observations, lessons, and advice, the fun stuff, I believe that it is necessary to define several types of projects and project structures. Because these definitions vary from industry to industry, they may appear different from the ones you are used to. Nonetheless, the definitions match my experience. I will also comment, for the benefit of the project managers, on the variations in complexity and difficulty in projects, depending on many factors.

Projects vary basically in the way their contracts are written; they also vary dramatically in complexity based on scope, the number of disciplines needed to supply the scope, schedule requirements, relationships between the participants, capabilities of the participants, as well as the geographical and political conditions to be encountered. Because of their difficulty and unique challenges, I will devote chapters of this book to turnkey and fast track projects (chapter 8) and so-called international projects (chapter 7).

There are three common methods for establishing the final price of a contract or subcontract: cost type, lump sum (or fixed price) type, and unit priced type. Although most contracts use a single method, large contracts are often made up of scope elements contracted in a combination of these methods. Each method has its own set of dangers and lessons to be learned.

Cost type contracts and subcontracts: In this type of contract, you (or your subcontractor) are paid what you spend. I would use this type only when the scope of work cannot be defined at the outset. This situation can occur when there is no time to develop and estimate a detailed scope of supply. Payments are made as the expenditures are incurred. The prime issue for the contracting party is to ensure that the money is properly spent and that value is achieved for the payments made. For the contractor, an important issue is the amount of the overhead and margin the contractor is paid, depending on the cost of the final scope of work.

I have seen contractors abused under this arrangement when agreeing to fixed fees on a poorly defined cost type contract, in which the owner expected to and did direct significant scope/cost growth.

A second problem for the contractor is when the owner (or contracting party) is, in the name of cost control, allowed to become involved in day-to-day decisions as well as in operational and personnel matters. Be careful, most contractors have better capabilities than the interfering and often biased contracting parties.

Lump sum or fixed price contracts or subcontracts: In this type of contract, you (or your subcontractor) are paid an amount agreed at the outset for the scope contracted for. The price of agreed-to changes is then added. Payments are typically made as progress is demonstrated or in accordance with an agreed-upon set of milestones achieved. The contracting party must ensure the scope is accomplished without contract changes developed only because the contractor is in cost trouble, avoid scope changes and scope disputes, and ensure that excessive payments are not made earlier than necessary. The contractor must manage cost (schedule is cost) and ensure that there is a written agreement with the owner to pay for any scope changes before the work is done and to pay for changes in conditions that affect the contractor's ability to perform.

Unit priced contracts or subcontracts: In this type of contract or subcontract, there is an agreed-upon value for each unit of quantities manufactured, installed, built, or erected (cubic yards of material or concrete, tons of steel, feet of pipe or cable). Payments are made as the quantities are installed. The issue here is for both parties to ensure that there is carefully checked agreement on the as-designed quantities and that only these amounts are installed and paid for. The contracting party must ensure that payment is for what is on the drawings, not what the contractor installs.

Projects can then be categorized based on their complexities. The simplest projects deliver a product from a single discipline, such as designs, software packages, or manufactured products (without supporting supply by others).

The next step up includes one or more supporting work elements supplied by internal supporting groups, contractors, or vendors. These elements are sometimes in sequence, supporting the primary activity. Engineering, procurement, or supporting fabrications fall into this category. These elements of the work should ideally be completed to the maximum extent possible before the next activity starts. I will refer to this project type as "extended scope," particularly when one division/department or company sells its product along with engineering, design, procured material, construction, or the like, supplied by others or a different part of the company.

Turnkey projects, the next step in complexity, include the multiple discipline scopes combined with whatever is necessary (testing, commissioning, and training) for the owner to immediately make productive and beneficial use of the product or system at project completion.

Managing these sequences and supporting work is made much more difficult when supporting activities overlap, for schedule acceleration. This brings greater opportunity for claims from or between the parties. This is typically called "fast tracking." I will address these two types of contracts in a later chapter.

Another variable in complexity is how detailed the definition of the project scope is. A conceptual scope or scope definition written around functional requirements has its own special risks. This approach is often used to accelerate the start of a contract when time cannot be taken to define the scope. While the functions to be satisfied can be agreed upon and accomplished, the detail in many design, engineering, or quality conditions will usually be the source of dispute, rework, and cost overrun. Neither party will have a strong contractual basis for its positions (unless the dispute involves one of the few detailed contract requirements).

This conceptual scope contract is particularly risky when used in a lump sum arrangement. The alternatives of unit pricing or cost type are certainly more compatible yet more risky for the contracting party.

I prefer a contract that defines the scope in detail. There is no uncertainty, and there will be minimal basis for dispute if either party seeks a legitimate change. The definition of detail in the design and engineering should not be troublesome or cause delays, as it often does when using a conceptual scope.

A project's complexity and difficulty can vary with location; language; social conditions; prevailing weather; accessibility; labor availability, cost, and organization; nature of the customer; and local business practices. These are only examples of variances to be managed. A construction project in Arkansas will have very different labor management issues than the same project in Boston. The weather issues of a project in Minnesota will usually require more cost and planning than one in Florida. Access to a construction site in Montana will present different challenges than one near the port of Houston, Texas.

Contracting with the US government or a highly structured corporation is usually more different than dealing with a small manufacturing company in rural Idaho. There are some differences in business practices within the United States that need to be understood, but these business practice complexities are usually apparent in the international arena.

I once visited an international construction site prior to the award of a contract to our company. I found no excuses for less than good performance. There was skilled low cost labor, good access, and adequate living conditions for our staff, no language issue, a sophisticated customer, and good year-round weather conditions. What more could we want? Surprise, our biggest local concern, by far, was the existence of a major "sin city" within driving distance. I missed it, and we routinely lost our staff, sometimes permanently, to whatever they did there. Providing recreation in remote locations is a costly necessity, but good judgments are critical.

In chapter 8 of this book, I will devote more time specifically to extended scope, turnkey, and fast track projects. In chapter 9, for Managers of Projects, I will discuss the complexities introduced in the structure of projects when deciding how to divide scope between different companies or parts of companies and how to relate these players contractually. Concepts of partnering, joint ventures, and simple subcontracting must be understood, particularly the risks and opportunities inherent in each.

These definitions are quite simple. "Extended scope" means multiple disciplines are involved. "Fast track" means that the work of the disciplines overlaps significantly and often have iterative processes between them. Turnkey projects have the added scope of turning the project over to the customer fully demonstrated, tested, and ready for immediate beneficial occupancy.

In closing this chapter on different types of project structures, let me comment on the issues I have observed with companies taking contracts for large multifunction projects. Project managers need to "watch out" when considering taking a project under these circumstances. Most companies taking contracts for larger multifunction projects are in it to make a profit on the scope of the project as a whole. Most of my experience is with companies who only take the large projects in order to sell the company's core engineering services, components, systems, or equipment, which would be a substantial portion of the project scope of work. Don't be fooled; the companies with this motive are as interested in the profit as anyone. On the other hand, they are generally less capable than the companies who specialize in larger multifunction projects. They are generally less capable because their culture, internal training, and internal systems, including sales, are oriented toward the supply of engineering, systems, or equipment and not the supporting scope necessary in larger projects. Additionally, the marketing and sales staffs of these engineering, equipment, or component companies are focused on the products or services that they primarily sell. They are generally not prepared to develop cost estimates and proper contract terms for the extended scope work. Moreover, they are generally willing to make concessions on cost and contract terms for the extended scope (the scope which is not their component, service or equipment) portion of the sale in order to sell their core product or service.

Another type of participants is what I call the opportunists. During periods of strong markets for projects in any field, these companies jump in, usually unprepared and inadequately staffed. This category includes those who seek to accumulate the necessary skills by forming a partnership with an entity that has not proven that it can either do the job or work together effectively. I would avoid taking project execution responsibility under such an arrangement.

Nonetheless, when the sale is made, all companies expect to achieve the margins and profit forecast when bidding the work. This leaves the responsibility with the project team, who will be measured by achievement of cost level in the company's initial estimate no matter what it was. My advice is to understand what you are taking on and not stake your future without a full understanding of the company's circumstances and their experience with the contract structure to be used.

CHAPTER 2.

TRAITS OF A STRONG PROJECT MANAGER

Is Your Glass Half Empty or Half Full?

Do you find yourself hoping for an outcome in one area of your project? If so, you are in the "Hope Mode," and that is not good. Not in this business. Not unless you have a contingency plan ready to go in the event that the outcome you hoped for does not occur. If in your everyday life you are consistently optimistic about the outcome of most situations, kind of hoping for the right outcome, I believe that you will have difficulty as a project manager.

Being prepared for the unexpected or the wrong outcome in any routine, but important, situation is critical to your success. I have observed that that preparation comes naturally to many managers; why, I do not know. I have tried to develop that trait in some project managers, but I have found it to be difficult, with real success only in a few cases. The trait, I concluded, was inbred, developed early in their career or long before they came to work.

Ultimately, in many cases as part of the training process, I would resort to an approach that I will discuss later in the chapter on information flow systems for managers of project managers. I would insist that project managers and their teams identify what they saw as issues critical to the customer's satisfaction, the project schedule, or the cost situation. In turn, a contingency plan would be required. Our success, however, was dependent on the team's internal honesty and the degree of transparency the team would allow. Some would, for whatever reason, never acknowledge that there was a problem or risk. The kimono would never be opened.

Such characteristics are easy to detect and require much more oversight by managers at the project level or above. Frankly, this more intense oversight is exactly what the individual was trying to avoid.

Having used this discussion as my cover story, I should, I suppose, devote more time. On the other hand, it is quite simple. If you do not anticipate problems and plan for them, you will clearly be in trouble. If vanity, pride, or just fear keeps you from acknowledging the realistic potential for problems, you will eventually be in trouble. If projects always ran as smoothly as we hoped, project managers would not be paid as much. The dropouts that I spoke of in the preface could easily do the job and remain happy ever after.

This trait is the single most important trait for a project manager looking for success.

Can You Tolerate Detail?

We all know very bright and capable people who will avoid as much detail as possible in their daily work. Many of them are successful if they have chosen the right position or place in the organization. Alternately, a good project manager must be willing and able to "dive in," not into everything, but to have a sense of where to start peeling back the layers of detail. This attention to detail is necessary in order to analyze a problem or follow up where you think a problem might be.

Later in the book, I will speak to processes of gathering information and monitoring progress. This process involves receiving written data, oral comment and facts, and even body language. I will also devote substantial time to finding variances from a well-made plan.

Anyone can become terribly bogged down in repetitive details, but the successful project manager will learn to use the information gathered routinely to pick the areas where it is necessary to penetrate the detail or ask deeper and deeper questions. The key skill is in picking the areas to penetrate so as to not get bogged down, and the key trait is a willingness to look at the detail. The ability to identify variances to detailed plans is absolutely critical.

Can You Be Open and Transparent with Good and Bad News?

Let me restate my strong position that a project manager must take the attitude that surprises, even apparently good ones, are to be avoided. Bad surprises are much worse when they are covered up, for whatever reason.

As a single example among many, I recall when a project manager held back some good surprises. He had negotiated favorable contract changes with the owner, was ahead of his schedule, overcame a technical risk that we had provided for, and had spent considerably less on a few major procurements. He wanted to be a hero and find significant recognition at the end of the project. In the interim we, in the project organization as a whole, were a little behind on our current margin/profit recognition forecast, as was the company as a whole. There was some risk that we might have to release some of our temporary staff to cut cost and improve our profits. If I had known about the surprise coming, I could have satisfied the company's needs and not sweat so much about the potential layoffs.

Needless to say, when Mr. Surprise finally came forward, he did not receive the recognition he and his team deserved for making the improvements in the first place. They received negative points as well as more oversight in the future.

Bad surprises are to be avoided, but at times they are inevitable. The key is to expose them. Being open allows more experienced or influential colleagues to help; it can also allow the larger financial unit to plan for the cost involved, sometimes saving embarrassment for all involved. Delaying and hoping for whatever reason is a formula for bigger trouble. I always had more respect for individuals with the courage to be open, even if they could have solved the issue alone.

Are You Free to Travel Away from the Office?

An effective project manager must spend time away from the office to see what is really going on, what people really think and to show their interest. I could never fully understand the reality of a project team using only reports and the telephone. Further, I am sure that while the newer videoconference technologies help, they are no full substitute for "pressing the flesh."

For the same reason, your relationship with your customer will be markedly better if you can talk directly. He will appreciate your interest and effort.

If for any reason a project manager or key team member is unable to travel regularly to visit customers, vendors, or a manufacturing or construction site, that individual should seek another project-related position (or even another vocation). There are many legitimate reasons preventing being able to travel. Family issues, health, personal anxiety about staying in an uncomfortable location can all be valid reasons not to travel. If the reasons are valid and prevent your travel, there is no shame, certainly less than the potential project failure.

When you travel, go, work hard, and get home. I made over sixty trips to Egypt in four years, never traveling south of the Cairo area, and saw the pyramids only twice (both times at night). Personal side trips aggravate the situation, especially when you call home from a resort in San Diego, Phuket, or a similar location. Your support from the home-front will dwindle.

It often made me angry when, while travelling on business and being crammed in a middle seat or sleeping in rural motels or even freight shipping containers, someone would ask about the glamour of my travel. I would travel across the country or halfway around the world to arrive just in time for my child's recital or a youth hockey game, because I believed what I am writing here. You cannot manage a sizable project from your office.

Are You Comfortable with Confrontation When It Is Necessary?

As a project manager, almost everyone, except your team, will seek to gain at your expense. It is a natural part of the business. Obviously, subcontractors and vendors are in this category. The supervisor supplying you with engineering services can gain by minimizing his or her efforts. The functional manager, supplying you with project staff, has somewhat different goals than yours.

Your customer can be very adversarial but will not be successful if the project does not succeed. I said the project, not you. Be cautions project managers can be replaced, and the project will go on. The terms of larger projects usually give the customer control of the assignment and tenure of the key project staff.

I have seen repeatedly where very capable people have not done well when it was necessary to step into a potentially confrontational, even adversarial, situation. Customers will delay payments or seek changes in scope that are not contracted for. Labor will seek to make new work rules. Subcontractors will seek claims or not perform to schedule. You, as the project manager, must be able to professionally address these issues and many more like them. If you are in any way uncomfortable with this, you may have difficulty leading a successful project team.

Are You a Team Player?

Throughout this book, I repeatedly refer to a project team. Even as an individual working a small project, you will by simple definition of a project be getting work done through others. First, always remember that you will never be successful if the project as a whole fails. As in most endeavors, your support cast can make you be successful or fail miserably, particularly when they support you but do not report to you directly. If you have been told that you are more suited as an individual contributor, or if you are more comfortable in that role, follow that path. There is nothing wrong with contributing as an individual. I know some very rich and happy individual contributors in many different companies.

Can You Take an Interest in the Accounting Side?

In more than one company, I encountered systems that rolled all project accounting into a single account/ledger. In chapter 9, I will address the importance of measuring and accounting for projects individually. The issue is important for the project manager as well. On one hand, the practice of a single measure can cover poor project performance. On the other, it will keep project managers from being recognized when there is good performance on their part.

My belief is that we are in the business to make money for our respective companies while ensuring that our customers are treated fairly under the contracts. We will not know if we are making money if we are not measured individually. As importantly, we will not be able to maximize the profit for the company unless we understand and make decisions consistent with the accounting system being used.

If you understand and work closely with the accounting staff, you can take steps such a matching the timing of revenue-earning milestones with the accounting cycle. You will ensure that decisions on contingencies and timing of ledger entries are in the best interest of the project, and you will match your cost-related plans and measures to the company's system.

You must be willing to learn as much about project accounting as about the legal intricacies of contract administration, scheduling, or labor/human relations.

CHAPTER 3.

CRITICAL ELEMENTS IN THE PROJECT MANAGER'S APPROACH

Plan and Manage the Variances

This is not a theoretical project management process manual, and I assume readers understand these basic processes and the supporting language. However, I must dwell on a few very important planning processes in order to develop my primary lesson, that is, the value of managing variances to a long-standing original plan for schedule, scope, and the cost of the project. I will stress the four interrelated processes of the project plan: the scope, the schedule, the cost of the work elements, and the plan for measuring the earned progress on the project. I have tried not to dwell on "how to" but to provide the logic for and the incentive to use these processes. I will also highlight some of the typical mistakes made.

Managing variances to plans requires starting with a very good plan. The overall project plan should be made up of a clear definition of the agreed-upon work scope, a detailed logic-driven schedule, a cost detail plan including a system for continuously estimating the cost at project completion (which is built on the Original Cost Estimate), and finally a system of measuring the earned progress using weighted work elements found on the logic schedule.

The latter is necessary because the schedule in itself focuses on specific activities and a critical path, but not the value (typically the cost) of what has been accomplished. For example, a project can, in the early stages, meet the critical path but be far behind in accomplishing the volume of nonscheduled critical work required. We would call this a "bow wave" or volume of work that would ultimately become the critical activity for the project overcoming the actual critical path in importance. Therefore, good schedule management requires a base plan composed of an integrated, logic-driven, detailed schedule and an earned progress system, which is based on the same integrated schedule with activities weighted with relative cost or man-hour values from the Original Cost Estimate.

I learned that, if there are good plans in these areas, I could simply measure the variances to the plans. This approach was critical to my personal time management as a project manager and as a manager of project managers. I knew where to spend my valuable time in either position. For example, as part of my reports (or the reports that I or the customer received), I never wanted a list of what was accomplished without a very careful listing of what was in the original schedule plan or earned progress plan that was not done. I knew that if the plan was good and that if I was told what was not done, I could pinpoint what it was that needed attention as well as what was done. Frankly, I did not care what had been done as long as we had a manageable list of where we needed to apply attention, the variance to the project plan. Specifically, we were identifying variances to our various plans so that we could focus on these variances.

Plan Number 1: The Scope Definition and Plan

Scope definition, with a documented agreement with your customer, is absolutely critical. One of the best ways to lose a good customer is to not insist on a clear statement of the work scope, either in the contract or in a separate agreement. On the contrary, I have had experience in the so-called "Good Old Boys" network that was prevalent in the electric utility industry in years past. The handshake was overused, and the supplier or contractor was the usual loser.

I strongly believe that there are three very good ways to achieve the required agreement. Begin with a very clear statement of the work in the contract. In doing so, be alert for the inclusion of scope elements elsewhere in the contract. I have had bad experiences with the customer or the salespeople putting scope elements in the general section or specific terms where one would not usually find scope elements. Sales people will do this to try to avoid including the cost in the project estimate. These terms are usually delegated to the legal folks for review. The legal department is not usually focused on scope; they often ignore the scope items, and the project people reviewing the proposed contract tend to avoid these areas of the terms and conditions.

I found that quite often certain functional or performance requirements were not put in the scope section of the contract. Examples of other scope requirements that are often hidden in the non-scope terms were the documentation to be provided, language to be used, formats and dimension requirements for drawings and other documents, training requirements, meeting attendance, special reports, control of your team by the customer, control of vendors, references to the customer's books of specifications, and travel and living expenses for the customer's staff.

If the contract is of the old handshake model, you must make every effort to build a mutually agreed, documented scope as soon as possible. It may take some time, but the scope definition and agreement are a must. If the contract is based on a concept only, be sure that the functional requirements are well documented and are not supplemented by other requirements that are not provided for in your cost estimate.

The second very important step in defining the project scope is to require a meeting with the sales team to turn over all documentation. The documentation must have a clear statement of where the scope is defined, along with a written statement on whether there are any other written, oral, or implied commitments of scope additions or changes. It is important to document this carefully, as more often than not; your customer will raise the issue of what else they were promised. Other subjects for the meeting agenda, such as the identified cost risks and opportunities, will be discussed in chapter 6 in the section on kicking off a project. In closing this meeting, the project manager should make it clear to the sales staff that they have no further authority to agree to changes in the scope (or any other part of the contract).

The final key step in scope planning is to meet early on with the customer in what I call a "kickoff" meeting. At this meeting, you should discuss and document agreement on many topics including but not limited to your plans for development of the project schedule, communications procedures and limitations, notices, change procedures, individual responsibilities and limits of authority, planned equipment sources and subcontracting plans, expectations for and compliance with all terms and conditions, and most importantly the scope of work. This is the time to bring out customer expectations for all elements of the documented scope, as well as their expectations for what is not documented. It is critical to take the time to discuss each element of the scope and functional requirements in order to ensure a mutual understanding and a sound basis for your planning.

After completing these steps, the project manager must take the time to communicate the final agreed-to scope of work to the entire team. I have had sad experience with team members who were not fully aware of the scope, agreeing to provide what was not to be supplied under the contract or objecting to supplying what was required by the contract. Costs were incurred unnecessarily, time was lost, or a customer was unnecessarily annoyed.

Plan Number 2: The Schedule Plan

As I said at the beginning, my goal is not to teach the mechanics of developing a schedule. I will, however, address the usual pitfalls or causes of failure in the planning process and the value of planning the work, measuring the progress, and focusing on variances that need attention. Once the scope is clarified, the schedule, typically with logic and constraints in the work sequence and weighted with a common measure of progress (or work to be done), is the next step in the overall planning process.

This section will, as with other sections, be structured around the most common mistakes and omissions in the schedule planning process.

Many managers will avoid developing a detailed and accurate schedule. The idea that "real men (or women) don't need critical path schedules" is usually some form of cover-up. There are those who are just plain lazy. There are those that down deep do not want to be measured against a schedule. Others will develop a schedule with milestones that are easy to achieve in the early stages of a project, allowing for apparent success, early contract payments from the customer, a good first annual bonus, or just an honorable escape to a new position or project during the early stages of a long project.

Good schedules come from tedious work. As I said, sometimes the team just wants to bypass that work.

However the schedule is developed, or which software is used, a critical issue is the ultimate ownership of the schedule by the project team. It is a mistake to assign the development of the schedule to a professional planner or the planning department while the team works on what they want to believe is the real work of starting up the project. It just cannot be done properly that way, and more importantly, there will be no ownership within the project team.

The schedule must be developed by a combination of individuals familiar with the project scope, the specific sequences and dependencies of the work elements to be performed and by individuals who are expert in the use of the computer application to be used to document the schedule. This collaboration is a must for accuracy and ownership by all.

The schedule must be complete through the absolute end and must be tied to the contract milestones and completion. I have seen managers satisfied with a schedule through part of the project, only to find that there is not enough time to finish. This approach is generally just plain procrastination, but often it is another "sleight of hand" with the intent of stretching out the early stages and avoiding criticism in the early going.

I mentioned in the preface that I was taught to never to compare my progress against a schedule without mentioning the revision date of the schedule that I was comparing to. Anyone can be on schedule when they can change the time-based plan, the schedule. As project manager, and later when I became responsible for many projects, I would insist that any reports from subcontractors, supporting groups, or project teams followed the same rule. The best way to avoid this conflict is to not change the schedule.

Remember my lesson from the Admiral. Schedules should only be changed when there is no other choice. By this I mean that there is no choice when the progress is so early or late that holding the dates for future milestones (equipment deliveries, subcontract placements, or contractor mobilizations and the like) would be costly to the project. These costs come in many forms. Contractor or vendor delay or acceleration costs to meet unnecessary milestones, storage costs for deliveries that are early, and salaries for idle time are a few examples. The team must be held to the original schedule as long as possible.

I also advise avoiding logic changes. While some logic change might be necessary, my experience is that the normal motive in making logic or sequence constraint changes is to lead to a false conclusion (for example, to demonstrate that the project is somehow on schedule when, in fact, it is well behind).

Another mistake, intentional or otherwise, is to create a superficial schedule with the intention of "developing it as you go." This approach is sometimes used to avoid the initial effort and sometimes is intended to provide for logic and schedule revisions that will get the project "back on schedule" when it inevitably falls behind. Schedules are superficial and useless when they are not well thought through or lack reasonable detail. Detail in all phases is a must. For example, a construction schedule for a large project will have elements numbered in the thousands. This activity count target does not include repetitive or duplicate elements for similar activities, a standard trick by many.

The work activities of supporting groups, engineering, procurement, and particularly subcontractors absolutely must be integrated. There is no sense at all in developing a schedule without complete buy-in and integration of the work done by supporting groups and subcontractors. Over and over again, I have seen project teams develop a schedule only to realize that the contractor, procurement staff, or engineering organization had different logic, sequences, and durations. Disputes then arise, driven by pride and a basic unwillingness to change and certainly a lack of overall ownership. Even if it takes time, the supporting groups must be required to develop accurate schedules, which the project team must work diplomatically but aggressively to integrate. There must be ownership by all.

A caution at this point, that I will elaborate on later: avoid pressing any of the supporting parties or subcontractors to agree to schedules that cannot be supported by some activities performed earlier in the project sequence by others, including your project team. As the lead and the project integrator, your project team will take a substantial risk of delay or acceleration claims coming from the accelerated contractor or other supporting party should your team or other supporting parties not meet the commitments promised. I have seen many cases where a project team pressed a contractor to an accelerated schedule, thinking that this was building in some valuable float to the contract milestones and maybe some "atta boys" from the boss. The contractor is usually approached with the idea of, "Let's try to accelerate, we will be no worse off if we do not make it." More often than not, the project team, other contractors, or other supporting parties will not be able to support the acceleration, and delay claims will result from the accelerating contractor.

A very good approach, in fact a must, is to supplement the basic schedule with a long "lists of lists" that my Admiral spoke of. Every discipline has list-able work that can be planned and have progress measured. Drawings, equipment or material deliveries, specifications, manuals, test documents, purchase orders, fabrications, and prerequisites to commissioning and operating milestones are a short list of possible list-able work elements that must be developed and tracked carefully. These lists must be tied, in logic and constraints, to the base schedule and should be developed before the particular phase of work is begun.

Lists with scheduled completion dates can usually be displayed as both plan and progress achieved in a graph format. I will describe these so-called "quantity progress curves" and discuss their value later in this chapter.

Yes, when it comes to the development of schedules, my glass is always half empty. As I said, I have been confronted with all sorts of poor schedules and unacceptable motives from those who are charged with developing the schedules.

Finally, on a complex project, the scheduled detailed activities must have accurate definition of their weight toward completion, using a common measure. This step is necessary to support an earned progress program, the fourth plan necessary for true management of variances. I will discuss the weighting of work activities later in this chapter.

Plan Number 3: The Cost Plan

The next step in planning necessary in order to ultimately manage variances is to be able to accurately develop a plan or forecast of the project's cost over time toward a cost at project completion. This is an absolutely critical step in the overall planning process. It is the baseline against which we measure the cost variances associated with the cost incurred and the value of the work completed, productivity in direct cost, the projected cost of the work at project completion, as well as the variances in the commitments made to changes in both the project direct and indirect costs. The cost plan is also essential in longer term projects in order to predict the cash flow required, project revenue (sales), and cost and margins (profit without company/profit center overhead burdens) over the project's duration.

Beyond the honesty and openness of the project team, there are several tools and concepts that are necessary for success in developing and maintaining the cost plan.

In order to be clear in this and the next two sections, I would like to explain my use of a few cost-related terms. I am avoiding the word "definition," in order to avoid arguments about my use of the terms, not my definitions.

Original Cost Estimate (OCE). Cost estimates for individual work elements and the total project cost from the pre-contract estimate for the project.

Forecast at Completion (FAC). The best estimate of the project cost at completion based on what has been learned at any point. that will cause changes to the Original Cost Estimate. These changes include commitments (see below) made, changes in the cost of work completed, cost of items procured, changes to the cost of planned work based on matters like bids for the work, subcontract change orders committed to, changes to the project indirect cost accepted schedule changes or anticipated change orders. Staffing level changes forecast are examples of committed changes to the project's indirect cost.

Remember, this forecast is not an extrapolation of cost actually incurred, that is amounts paid out and booked in the company's financial ledger. The FAC is based on both actual cost incurred, costs outside the OCE that have been committed, and cost changes that can be forecast using analysis of relevant data, such as the productivity of the work force.

Commitment. A commitment is the result of an action by a team member to change the direct or indirect cost of the project from the original estimate. Accounting for commitments is very important, even if the actual cost is not yet incurred. Commitments are often overlooked when compiling the FAC.

Cost Forecast Curve (CFC). This curve is a time-based projected estimate of the actual cost to be incurred over time, which must be synchronized with the FAC. It is initially developed by applying cost from the OCE to the same elements of work in the schedule plan and is updated as the FAC is updated. Commitments to cost changes must be forecast at the time the cost will be incurred.

Curve of Actual Cost. This is a curve of the actual cost as it is incurred over time, which is generally compared to the FAC. The actual costs should be compiled against the same breakdown of the work elements that were used in the OCE.

Direct Cost. This is simply the cost of procuring and doing the work described under the project scope.

Indirect Cost. This is the cost incurred by the prime project team in performing the project. As examples, their burdened labor, travel and living, field office costs, their procured services and equipment, insurance, and subcontracted project staff fall in this category. Other costs, such as the cost of the company's cash flow investment in the project, are added on a case-by-case basis. Company overhead, which is typically the difference between the project margin and the project profit, does not fall into this category.

The first step in cost planning is to develop the FAC. This plan is not time based like the schedule but is a continuous update of the OCE as the project proceeds, taking advantage of what has been learned.

At this point, a caution is necessary. Often a project team will not accept or take ownership of the Original Cost Estimate. This is unfortunate but certainly not a reason, under any circumstances, to adjust the cost for elements of work in the plan. As with the schedule, teams will often attempt to increase cost provided for work done early in the project or to give stretch cost targets to others. The motives would be similar. If the pre-contract procedure included a review by the project manager, the issue should not come up. If not, the OCE just has to be accepted by the project manager and the team as a condition of their assignment to the project. I never liked this situation, but the company cannot tolerate a team working to and owning a different cost and profit plan for the project.

The plan should be at least as detailed as the OCE and provide for some contingency. The pre-contract estimate should have provided for a cost contingency, generally over the objection of the sales staff. The contingency is quite important, because bad stuff inevitably happens. To make room for a realistic contingency in the cost plan, it might be a good idea to use any cost under-runs identified early instead of reducing the FAC. This is the only change to the OCE that I would allow in finalizing the baseline for the FAC. I will comment on the management of contingencies near the end of this chapter.

For small fixed price work elements or procurements, the process is easy. Simply compare the value of the procurement placed or work element completed with the OCE. There is, however, a caution. If you base your forecasted cost on the value of the procurement or the subcontract placed, you might want to provide, in your forecast, for the inevitable change order.

Since indirect costs are, at least in part, based on the duration of the project, any change in the anticipated schedule must be considered when updating the FAC. Indirect staff levels are another often missed cost change. When additions are made to the project team with the intention of maintaining the additions, then that is a commitment of the cost, which must be recognized in the FAC. I have always encountered difficulty with teams or individuals who cannot grasp the idea that these changes to planned indirect cost are commitments that must be reflected in the FAC at the time when the commitment is made, not when the cost is actually incurred in the future.

Another example of a commitment that should be added to the FAC currently is direction to your work force, a subcontractor, or supporting party to do work in the future that will add cost beyond the OCE. Here again, the time for the FAC change is when the commitment is made, not when the cost is eventually incurred.

Unless the concept of the commitment is understood and committed cost changes are included in the FAC currently, the FAC is of little value and the project will encounter big surprises later.

The ability to measure productivity in the early stages of each element of project work is another very valuable tool when maintaining an accurate FAC. As work begins in an area of work, the actual cost of the work accomplished can be related to the expected cost of that amount of work using the Original Cost Estimate. This cost can be measured in currency or the relationship between man-hours planned and man-hours expended. A simple division will yield a productivity rate that can be compared with the productivity rate used in the Original Cost Estimate. Allowing for a startup learning curve, the productivity rate comparison provides an accurate basis for forecasting the final cost of the work element. Clearly, analysis of the productivity within early work activity can be used to make some early judgment about the long-term productivity of the work force involved and importantly be the basis for defining a variance to be addressed.

Another value of continually updating the FAC is in tracking the trend in your forecasts over time. A curve plotting your estimates of FAC over time is often very telling in itself. I will always remember managing my first very large project, a government contract. I was representing the government as project manager on a cost-based contract. I came to know that the government placed the contract at a low target cost in order to keep the contractor's fee low, but expected higher cost to be incurred. My team's job was to understand what the cost situation was, try to minimize the cost growth, and find sources in the various congressional appropriations to fund the final cost.

Knowing the final cost was the most important cost-related task; each month, we would look at cost increases we knew of and guess (or approximate) the FAC. After a few months, my boss predicted a much higher cost at completion. He had simply plotted my estimates from several months of reports against time and extrapolated the resulting S-shaped curve to its asymptotic flat point and said, "That's the cost to provide for." This was so simple and was all from our ever rising but inaccurate FACs. It was a lesson in both the proper development of and the uses of the FAC that I would never forget.

Beyond the FAC, the continuous updating of the onetime cost at the completion of the project is a planning technique that is of value in further analyzing variances to the overall project plan.

A Cost Forecast Curve is developed by attaching the elements of the OCE to the schedule of the work activities to be performed over time. The result is a time-based forecast of costs to be incurred. For some elements of the OCE, it might be necessary to obtain time-based cost breakdown data from contractors and supporting parties. Naturally, as the FAC is changed, the Cost Forecast Curve must be adjusted.

There are many values of such a curve. The CFC can be used to plan cash outflow. Cash inflow and overall cash flow can be added based on the customer's payment terms and planned progress. As I said, your company will use the CFC to plan for any cash flow that to be invested in the project. Be sure there is a plan to pay your project obligations. Depending on how your company books the project's revenue or sales to the company ledger, the cost curve may be of value. More selfishly, the project manager can use the CFC to analyze trends in cost versus schedule to help confirm or discredit the project's FAC. In like manner, the CFC, being the plan for actual cost to be incurred, can be compared with the actual cost of the work completed. This comparison will allow the team to visualize variances at any point in time or to visualize trends that must be addressed.

As I said, to be useful, the CFC must be based on the same breakdown of work as in the schedule, which should in turn match the breakdown in the OCE. Better yet, since the cost estimate came first, the schedule and cost plans should use the work breakdown from the cost estimate.

Summarizing, when analyzing the cost situation, there are three curves/calculations that should be used. The first is the CFC, which we have discussed. The second, the Curve of Actual Cost incurred (CAC), is the curve/calculation representing the actual cost incurred against time. The third is a time-based measure of the cost earned through earned progress. This third set of curves/calculations related to earned value or cost (actual progress) will be discussed in the section on managing variances.

The comparison of actual cost incurred with the CFC is of somewhat limited value, particularly when the scheduled progress is ahead or behind the schedule plan, introducing a third variable. On the other hand, the two curves can be very useful when used in combination with the schedule and earned progress data in curve format.

In closing on the subject of cost planning, I would like to stress the importance of assigning a trained cost engineer to all large projects. Even if shared with another project, this function, if disciplined with a strong dose of controllership, will be necessary. The individual should ideally be trained in accounting principles and controllership but is not the project accountant. He or She must be willing to be open and honest no matter what pressures are brought.

This individual must be fluent with the OCE and should develop the FAC as well as the CFC and be responsible for maintaining the FAC and actual cost calculations for the project manager. On the other hand, the engineer must report to a functional manager responsible for his or her training. This relationship is discussed later in chapter 9 on project organization. .Having someone familiar with maintaining an accurate forecast under pressure avoids undue influence from other members of the project team.

Cost Risks and Opportunities: A Cost Subplan

I believe that there is another absolutely necessary tool in the effort to both ensure an accurate forecast of completion cost and be prepared for any surprises related to the cost of the project. It involves an effort to identify risks to the cost plan and the project cost at completion. Often project teams will be aware of potential bad news (and, yes, even some potentially good news). The question then becomes how to handle this awareness with respect to the forecast of completion cost and the impact on the company financials as the project proceeds.

The risks and opportunities will not fall under a particular menu or list of cost categories. They require thought and, more importantly, honesty and transparency. Contract claims or changes from above or below in the contract hierarchy can be risks or opportunities. Failure to meet technical or performance requirements, unexpected taxes or fees, the need for larger staff size, potential extensions in the schedule, labor unrest, and late deliveries from vendors are a very short list of what could be costly risks.

Actually, the effort to identify these so-called cost risks and opportunities should begin during the pre-contract or sales phase. As I will discuss in chapter 6, the process of reviewing the suitability of a bid or contract requires a commitment to think through and if possible quantify the potential risks and opportunities. These risks and opportunities should also be given a realistic estimate of their probability, so that the potential cost risk in the sale and resultant margin can be accurately assessed.

I have found, as you might expect, the sales staff will be reluctant to realistically identify the risks, and if they do, they will assign a probability of "low." This would often spark a dispute with project or operations people who have to implement the contract. As in the case of the cost estimate, senior management will downplay the risks in favor of the sale, and the project team will then be measured by their ability to overcome the risks.

When the contract is signed and the work begins, a smart project team will make a strong and continuing effort to document and reassess the probability of the risks and opportunities. Two benefits will accrue.

First, the team will be continually reminded of the risks that must be focused upon and avoided with advanced planning. This same effort by the team will increase the possibility of realizing the cost saving opportunities.

The second benefit would be to place a band of uncertainty around the current project forecast at completion. This positive or negative band, if treated properly, could support a more aggressive or more conservative approach to booking the cost and margin for long-term projects into the company's ledger. A long-term project in this context is a project where the duration of project activity, and therefore the booking of revenue and cost, is longer than the period between ledger closings by the company (typically monthly or quarterly).

At one point, I had the opportunity to experience a third direct benefit. As manager of the project organization during a time when our company was being bought (or merged as some would say out of pride), we had developed a strong menu of the risks and opportunities for all our projects. Naturally the acquiring company wanted to assert that the risks we faced were potentially much more costly than we believed in order to force the price of our company down. The fact that we had maintained the menu of risks and had managed the risks for some time brought a degree of credibility, which was difficult to overcome by the acquiring company. Ultimately our stockholders were happy but the acquiring company was not. On the other hand, I expected that I would have to swallow the poison pill presented by the acquiring company. That never happened. In fact, they recognized the value of our processes.

On the other hand, the existence of a list of the risks and opportunities can be abused. I have seen many cases where auditors believe that that the risks have been understated and insist on adjustments to increase cost, thereby reducing the margins to be booked on the company ledgers in order to hedge these risks. I have also seen project teams purposefully understate the risks and overstate the opportunities, for obvious reasons. Likewise, company senior managers and financial managers will do the same in order to maximize the margins during an interim financial period.

Finally, I should address the inevitable question of how to treat the probabilities that the team has assigned to the risks and opportunities. I do agree that if I have confidence that an honest effort has been made, the risks and opportunities can be offset in the final analysis. While I am always skeptical of risks labeled as low, I will usually support weighting the value of the individual risks and opportunities with the assigned probabilities in an effort to summarize the financial impact during the course of the project. I see this approach as statistically quite reasonable only when there are a large number of risks and opportunities.

Cost Variance Tracking: A Cost Subplan

At one point just after I joined an organization, I recall a division manager continually asking, "Where the bleeding was when reviewing the costs." I remember thinking that was a great question, but no one could provide a reply, other than vague, general, and usually defensive answers. After thinking a while, I commissioned a bright, computer-savvy staff member to build a system so that we could answer the question. It would be nice to answer the question, but more importantly to me, I felt that if I had a good quantitative answer, I could set priorities and find solutions to the cost issues.

The task was not easy to complete and even more difficult to implement. Many did not want the answers to be exposed. In fact, after our new system was well implemented, the company's leaders turned against the system. They were no longer able to just blame cost overruns on the project's organization. The spotlight and heat spread to product and system engineering, procurement, manufacturing, and, yes, even sales.

As I will elaborate in chapter 6, what we did was to track cost changes by linking the various change orders, document changes, purchase order changes, rework notices, requests for manufacturing or engineering information, and the like to a responsible party, with totals linked using a computer application. We insisted that each team use the FAC process to match the cost totals to the cost changes encountered. It worked, and we could report and trend the data.

I strongly recommend, on complex projects, expanding the cost tracking system to link the cost of every cost variance to a root cause and responsible party. Corrections can then easily be prioritized and acted upon.

Don't worry about the extra work for the project staffs. They must be objective but will enjoy not being blamed for all of cost growth. They will enjoy answering the division manager's question in detail. The new question will be, "Does he or his staff want to know?" He might have to take actions outside the project organization.

Plan Number 4: The Earned Progress Plan

The final recommended plan is to measure the earned progress. The integrated logic-driven schedule is a mandatory ingredient of a successful large project plan, but from my experience it must be supplemented with an earned progress program. Most good computer-based scheduling applications can support such a system.

I have been told routinely, by project team members that they were meeting the critical path requirements. Being questioning by nature, and a pessimist, I looked at whatever they had for an earned value system and found that completion on time was improbable if not impossible. Up until just about halfway through the project, it is easy to concentrate solely on the critical path and leave so much "bulk" work behind that the volume of bulk work eventually becomes critical. If one looks at the current rate of overall work progress and compares that rate with the rate of earned value required to meet schedule, the answer will be obvious.

Applying earned progress to the basic project schedules is valuable as well. Different types of projects will have different possible and average achievement rates based on complexity and supply conditions. For example, most projects in the power plant construction business could sustain a maximum monthly rate of progress of about 10 percent. This was generally driven by space and sequence restraints. On the contrary many subcontractors would insist that they could perform or recover at a faster rate. It never happens.

The measure is primarily against the scope of direct project work but can include indirect cost under some circumstances. The system is built using the same computer-based application that has the schedule. Using the same work breakdown used by the OEC and the schedule and weighting the individual activities in the schedule with its percentage of the total cost, a time-based planned progress curve can be developed. The common weighting can be cost, man-hours, or the equivalent as long as it is a common work element and adds up to the FAC for the project.

Typically the resultant planned progress when plotted is some form of an S-shaped curve, allowing for a startup or learning period and a completion phase, where work is specific and limited in volume. As I mentioned above, a project manager experienced in a particular type of project scope will know the practical limits on the shape of the planned progress curve and rates of progress that can reasonably be forecast.

The benefit is derived when the actual progress is compared with the plan and the variances are observed. The actual progress is calculated by applying the associated weight to completed work activities and adding the earned weights for a total progress value, which can then be plotted against time. This same technique can be applied to similar types of work activities.

On many occasions early in a project, a supporting group, work force, or subcontractor would obviously be behind but would argue that the critical path was within sight and all was okay. With a quick look at the planned forecast progress curve, actual progress achieved, and future earned progress requirements, it would be obvious that they were in trouble and that urgent action was required by them and by my team to work around their probable lateness. The value of the system was clear. The system was often the one tool that would convince the party that was behind to take action.

As in most systems, there are good questions about how to handle certain situations and many ways for those who want to abuse the system in their favor to do their thing.

The weighting is my first concern. When people want to look good early or contractors are to be paid based on earned progress, their approach will be to weight the earlier activities heavier. This might be recognized by an experienced individual looking at the proposed curve or by comparing the weighting with the OCE or the bid data from a subcontractor. If the subcontractor is being paid on measured progress, you know the proposed weighting will be skewed.

Next, I would advise breaking the work activities into as small a unit as possible, in size and particularly in duration. If this is not possible, then set up a subsystem for that activity. A large volume of concrete, weight of weld to be laid, or drawings to be produced are examples of where such a subsystem might be applicable. In some cases, such as issuing a large number of documents through an iterative process of drafts and approvals, the progress value can be applied using the weight of an interim milestone.

Never use elapsed time or elapsed percentage of scheduled duration for an activity to determine weighted progress. I have seen this approach attempted with both direct and indirect work activities. If the project is credited with 50 percent of the concrete poured halfway through the planned interval, and 75 percent of the material is actually installed, there is an error. Most debate comes with its application to the value of indirect earned. Crediting 50 percent of the progress for the staffing of the project team or the indirect facilities cost when the project is at the halfway point of the original schedule is usually folly. There must be adjustments to reflect your current projection of the time of project completion.

When implemented, the earned progress variance evaluation will bring about the same simple conclusions as the actual schedule variances will, but the method is much more simple and convincing. Earned progress also allows for a simple extrapolation of the actual data in order to give a good idea of when the project work will really be complete.

Frankly, the best test of the accuracy of your proposed earned progress plan comes when it is too late. I have seen many projects come to about 90 percent and move flat or even negative for far longer than originally planned from that point. I have learned the lesson too many times, and many project managers have lost credibility under such circumstances. The weightings were obviously an internal lie.

Here, as in the cost area, for larger projects I would advise assigning an independent scheduler from a functional group to objectively build the plan and measure the progress for the project manager.

Quantity Progress Curves: An Earned Progress Subplan

A simpler but similar technique to the overall earned progress system is what I call the use of quantity curves. I mentioned this technique earlier in this chapter under the schedule plan after mentioning the use of lists, an even simpler but non-time-based approach. It is applicable to all forms of similar or equally weighted work activities performed over a longer period of time and measures progress with these activities without stressing weighting and the value of the progress.

The approach is simpler because one can imply a plan curve, knowing the total count of the activities and the planned duration. I say "imply," because with a little experience one can assume a progress curve typically with the common "S" shape. Progress against the planned curve, the plan, is then measured by counting the items completed. Data and trends can be extrapolated to final completion of similar activities.

On a typical extended scope power project, which included construction, we would have benefited from twenty-five or more of these curves. We applied them to procurement activities, engineering deliverables, fabrications, volume of concrete, bulk welds, pipe joints, cable installation, cable terminations, test procedures completed, subparts of these elements, and many more. Variances to plan were easily seen, and the system was so simple that it was difficult to evade the results.

These techniques are simple, but don't panic early on. Remember the progress is typically slower and the productivity lower at the start. On the other hand, don't wait too long and start hoping. If the input is good, what you see is real, and you must act. Contractors and supervisors will come up with all sorts of excuses and promises, but you should act on poor results before it is too late.

Managing Variances

In the discussions of the schedule, cost, and earned progress, I used comparisons between the plan and the actual data, usually visually displayed in curve format, to illustrate variances between the plan and the actual performance. This is basic variance identification, allowing project managers to focus their time and attention where it is needed most. As I said, this management of variances to plan is my most important lesson for both the project manager and the manager of project managers.

Schedule Variances

I believe that the discussion under plan 2 is adequate. If planned and actual schedule curves are used alone, then there are no special tricks or nuances in the schedule variance area.

Cost Variances

Evaluating cost variances is almost as simple if the planned cost and actual cost data is used alone. However, the cost curves can be used in conjunction with the schedule or the earned progress data to confirm or invalidate variances that might need attention. As an initial example, all variances between the curves for actual cost incurred and the OCE at any point in time are not bad or good, as might be quickly concluded. Actual cost can be low at any point in time, and not be a variance, if the scheduled progress is behind by a roughly comparable amount. The schedule would be the variance of concern in this circumstance. Actual cost can likewise be satisfactorily high if ahead of schedule without a negative variance in either case.

In like manner, the actual cost curves can be used in conjunction with the earned progress data. If the cost expended is higher in percentage than the earned progress, there is a cost variance or productivity issue of concern. On the contrary, there may be a future cost opportunity if the actual cost data is lower than the actual earned progress.

Earned Progress Variances

As I discussed under Plan 4, variances between the progress earned and the true progress variance planned can be quite straightforward, making clear the true progress in the "bulk" or noncritical path work on the project. Because it is built on the project schedule variances, the earned progress variance will also be seen, but not as clearly, from the schedule variance.

Productivity

At the risk of being overly repetitive, I would like to remind the reader that using actual cost incurred data and earned progress, specifically the quantity curves in like work activity, will yield a measure of productivity that can be compared to your or a subcontractor's initial estimate assumptions. For example, comparing the actual cost/man-hour spent with the progress achieved in issuing drawings or pulling cable will yield a productivity factor that can be compared with the original estimate. This productivity comparison will be very useful in both initiating corrective action and in projecting future cost risks or opportunities.

Management of Contingencies

The management of the contingencies, once established, is one of the best games played on a project. The games are typically played between the project team and their managers, senior executives, and financial departments. There is no single answer or strategy for winning the games. I can only tell you what to watch out for and that there will be conflicting interests to deal with.

The first round is establishing a proper value for contingency in the project estimate and subsequent bid. Sales and sales-oriented management "compliment" the team's skill by suggesting minimal or no contingency, but the project team wants as much cushion as possible. There are norms in various companies, but I believe that the contingency should include a modest amount for the inevitable and also provide a reasonable amount to cover the risks/opportunity package that should be objectively determined.

The next round is in determining what to do with cost savings or overruns: hide the change, add to or remove from contingency, or even book the change immediately as in increase or decrease in the margin at the company level. Chapter 2 expressed my opinion on surprises and transparency, so you know how I feel about hiding change. The other decisions must be made with good judgment for the best interest of the project and not special interests, the will of auditors, or the will of those higher in the management chain. Sure!

There is no single good answer. The answers are dependent on the stage of the project, the remaining contingency available, the remaining risks and opportunities, and even the credibility of the project team. The key is to understand the principle motive behind any proposed answer.

A similar game will involve the question about when to book all or part of the remaining contingency as the project progresses. Here again, there is no single answer beyond good judgment in the interest of the project.

CHAPTER 4.

CONTRACT ADMINISTRATION AND PRIME CONTRACT MANAGEMENT

Administration in General

Before addressing the management of your contract with your customer (in this chapter) and of your subcontractors (in the next chapter), I will make a few comments on often missed or disregarded topics in the discipline of contract administration in general.

Contract management must be recognized as a process that begins with the decision to bid a project; it continues through the bidding process into the execution, the closeout, and the warranty phases. Execution includes the disciplines of claim avoidance, change control, claim management, and warranty management.

Contract management begins with the project team's senior management. It is imperative that the company maintain and implement both procedures for bid control and standards for acceptable risks and contract terms. Bid control includes a process for deciding whether or not to bid a project and a process for evaluating and approving the bid to be made. This latter process must consider and measure legal, commercial, technical, and implementation risks against the standards set by the company. It must also define the level of management or executive approval required as a function of the level of the risks.

I have said, and will say again, it is imperative to know your contract and ensure that every member of your teams know the contract. I suggest that you meet and discuss anything in the contract that is in any way unusual; your team should be required to read and acknowledge, with a signature, the entire, yes, the entire, contract. I stress the entire contract because the authors often have reasons to hide terms or move them to where you would not expect them.

I stress all members of the team because I worked with a company where project management responsibility was divided between a commercial or contract manager and the project implementation manager. It was silly, beyond the concept of individual responsibility, which I believe in; people decided that they were on one side or another and were not required to understand or feel accountable for each of what they saw as two parts of the contract. I refused to comply with this approach.

You can promote knowledge and understanding of the contract by using, whenever possible, your company's standard terms and conditions of sale or purchase, if applicable. I say "whenever possible" because many buyers will have their own terms, which they will use to seek bids and will insist on using as the basis of contract negotiations. On the other hand, as the buyer, you can always insist on using your terms when subcontracting or buying.

My next concern is with the trained resources you need to properly administer the contract. In my first position managing a project management group, I inherited a culture where there were more contract administrators available to be assigned to project teams than there were schedulers or cost engineers. People paid attention to administering the contracts in order to ensure that the customer and the project team met their respective obligations and the subcontractors were managed so as to avoid claims.

Later, I joined a company where the only contract administrators were assigned to the pre-contract activities, that is, the processes of negotiating the contracts and finding a way to get management approval of any or all risks involved in the sale. This was a difficult and troublesome situation. At this company, I found more contract disputes than I thought were necessary.

Unfortunately, the subsequent task of hiring a staff of contract administrators for the project execution phase was equally difficult. We could not find a good source or an education program geared to the skill we needed. We found an abundance of so-called "quantity surveyors," a related, essentially European profession, who wanted the work but had a different skill set. We wanted people who were familiar with the application of our standard terms and conditions and who had a real sensitivity to the possible development of contract and subcontract disputes and who knew how to negotiate and write contract changes that were neutral and, if possible, in our favor.

That brings me to the training and qualifications necessary. I did find that most law firms and companies that specialize in developing or defending claims, who will represent you for exorbitant rates, will be willing to provide material or lead seminars for your staff. These materials and seminars are typically at no cost as long as you intend to use the firm in the event that you need outside legal assistance. While generic, these materials and seminars can readily be supplemented by training done by functional managers using your internal procedures where possible; I discuss this in chapter 9.

The lesson, therefore, is to retain a staff of administrators skilled and experienced in true contract administration.

From here, I will not attempt to play lawyer or address individual terms or sections of a contract. I will limit my discussion to several basic practices, which I have found to be helpful but also difficult to have project team members follow. Control of the team's communications is highest on my list. To start, let me say that communications technology has caused trouble for good project contract administration. Frankly, in the years before I retired, I would not allow the use of e-mails with external parties, that is our customers and our subcontractors. E-mails are too easy to fire off in a burst of emotion, bypassing the contractually prudent review process. There is no worse feeling during a negotiation or dispute than having your opponent produce an unfavorable e-mail or document that was not properly reviewed.

I believe that all outgoing and incoming correspondence should be reviewed by someone with a contract administration background.

For outgoing correspondence, this review is to ensure that the correspondence does not violate any of the terms of the contract and does not unknowingly impact the scope of the contract; it also ensures that unnecessary emotions have been eliminated. This review is important for correspondence with both your customer and your subcontractors. When consulting as an expert witness during arbitration cases, I was often shocked by the tone of correspondence between the parties. The words and tone obviously contributed to poor and unproductive relationships between the parties. I concluded that the inappropriate correspondence had a negative effect on the arbitration panel members. Most members of arbitration panels were as affected by their impression of the character of the parties as by the law and the facts of legal documents.

At one point, I had a site manager who responded in writing to a letter from his customer, saying briefly that the letter would "receive the attention that it deserved." Needless to say, it took me months to regain any form of credibility with that customer. The manager stayed on with our company but we required his subsequent communications to be reviewed before being released. In another case, a project team member found it fun to annoy a customer by routinely misspelling the customer's name. No matter how serious any dispute might be every effort must be made to keep all communications at a professional level.

My personal rule was that all outgoing written correspondence be reviewed by an independent party, typically the contract administrator, who was familiar with the contract and sensitive to trends and to language that could lead to disputes. This rule applied to all correspondence, including procurement, engineering, quality control, and routine "back and forth" communications. For incoming correspondence, I required that the formal communications be reviewed by an individual with the skills and background that I noted above. Certain language was often a tip-off to an intended claim or dispute of some kind.

On larger projects involving engineering or construction, there will be substantial communications in the processes of seeking or granting approvals or answering questions from or making clarifications to subcontractors. There can be a considerable volume of correspondence here, and the need for quick turnaround requires that it be handled at the project implementation site. This presents real challenges in a contract administration and claim avoidance sense. First, I would have, in place, standard written processes/procedures for the various types of correspondence. Engineers and junior staff are often insensitive to the impact of their communications. I would always insist on some form of one-over-one review prior to issue. I learned this early on when the owner of a large project required that I as project manager personally review all engineering instructions to and communications with a large subcontractor. This was my first lesson in how engineers tinker, want continuous improvement, and are never finished, a topic that I will address later in this book.

The sheer volume of correspondence can also be a concern with this type of communication. In managing projects and during dispute resolution, I have seen this type of routine and often high volume correspondence repeatedly used to the disadvantage of the issuing party. The receiver would disregard the content and argue that the number of communications clearly indicated some form of abuse or general scope change.

If a dispute with a subcontractor arises, a lawyer could simply count the volume of correspondence of any type and argue that there were too many questions or directives, that the number of questions or directives were evidence of a poor initial definition in the form of drawings or specifications, that there were excessive changes, or that there was defective material or equipment. The lawyer will argue that the volume constituted a direct scope change and that it required an increase in the indirect staff of the contractor involved. You will be hard pressed to justify each piece of correspondence. You should have your team minimize correspondence and combine communications whenever you can.

Another concern with a high volume of communications is that a backlog of required responses could accumulate, or some responses may not provide a satisfactory answer. Claim-minded administrators or lawyers will simply track the time intervals from issue to response and will claim for a delay impact, even if there would be no reasonable impact. Certainly this approach of prompt response applies to all communications.

Aside from the contractual risks, prompt and professional communications is good business and promotes good working relationships. You as the project manager should maintain a system for monitoring the age of required responses.

Next let me address the importance of complete and accurate documentation of the events, transactions, and agreements. I have observed in disputes that parties who acted in accordance with the contracts often lost in dispute resolution because they did not maintain documentation that would have supported their position. I have found myself in the same position when negotiating a contract settlement and finding that the project team had been too busy (or lazy) to document the proceedings properly. Yes, it is time consuming and a nuisance, but careful documentation is absolutely critical.

Certain documentation is particularly important. Signed documents beat handshakes when agreements are made. I remember when one subcontractor was about to go bankrupt, their lawyers took control of the project, and what had been a minor dispute suddenly changed, at least from their point of view. Fortunately, I had asked for and had received a letter from an honorable senior individual with the contractor. The letter clarified that our company was not responsible for the difficulty the subcontractor was having. That letter ultimately saved our company millions when the subcontractor filed what we believed to be a fraudulent claim, seeking to "split of the baby" in arbitration. Documenting agreements may be a little awkward at times, but insist on it and do it yourself.

Document the minutes of all meetings, twice if necessary. I say "twice," because at times I found that the other party would object to clear documentation and write a watered-down version. In this case, write and file your version documenting why you did so and formally copy the other party. At one point early in my career, I was dealing with a much more senior party representing the subcontractor, whose style was to appear not to take matters seriously, give only lip service to many issues, and certainly not allow time for meeting minutes, which would cause him to be held to agreements made. I knew that if the difficult situation was to continue, one of us would likely be dismissed by the ultimate customer. I decided to go to the next meeting with a draft of the minutes prepared. Every issue was defined, and the responses I wanted were clear. At the conclusion of the meeting he was forced to agree to most of the unambiguous documentation he had agreed to during the meeting. As it turned out, he was replaced and not I.

Another very important step is to document oral communications, particularly agreements of any sort with the other parties. This again can be awkward, but it is worth it. Always send the other party a copy. At the project manager's level, you can allow for an occasional off-the-record communication when you, not others, feel that it will help make progress on a particular issue. Keep these communications to a minimum. In this case, you should never expose your project or company to risk by implementing any off-the-record agreements until these agreements are documented.

Finally, you should develop procedures to ensure that all documents are readily retrievable when necessary. All project documents and written communications should have some form of indexing and be safely stored. Here again, the key is to develop strong procedures and train your staff to comply with them at all times.

I have seen case after case where the project team, who did not want a dispute but was forced into one, was very thankful that they documented the disputed issue and saved the documentation carefully for easy recovery.

In the paragraphs above, I used the term "sensitivity" when describing the skill of being alert to trends or words used in correspondence that signal the writer's intent to submit a claim or change order at some point. Yes, there are long menus of techniques used to support a later claim. For example, when a subcontractor refused to provide the cost or schedule impact of very minor changes, I could see a claim coming for the volume of small changes or asking for an increase in indirect cost in addition to the direct cost. Terms like "reserving rights" are other alerts. This sensitivity on the part of the reviewer of all correspondence can save you time and money by developing early response strategies.

When I saw that subcontractors were reserving rights or withholding statements on impacts, I would insist on periodic signed statements describing any unresolved disputes or claims the subcontractor had or was considering. I would insist on this as part of a required monthly written report. Alternately, I would use a structured part of a periodic meeting to require a statement listing any unresolved disputes or claims. These approaches were not foolproof but often worked to my advantage.

The Contract with Your Customer

In chapter 6, I will discuss your relationship with your customer, focusing on different customer attitudes, personalities, and cultures; your communications; and the differences in business practices you will encounter. In chapter 7, I will make a few points that are unique to international customers. In this section, I will build on the previous section on general administration, commenting on the types of customers to be prepared for and suggesting a few administration techniques particular to your customer.

Different customers have different cultures, which results in different approaches to managing contracts. There are frequent buyers, who are very knowledgeable about your type of product and may have their own detailed contract terms and technical specifications. These customers typically have large staffs overseeing your every move. Next, there are first-time buyers, who may be more willing to stand back and use your ideas and recommendations, or they may hire a third party to oversee your work. This third party, used extensively in international projects, is typically a generalized contract manager, who will manage you with very generic procedures (not good) and as many people as they can scare the customer into paying for. Normally, this contractor will continually seek to prove himself to the customer at your expense. In chapter 6 in the section on relationships with your customer, I provide some more advice on dealing with aggressive or interfering customers.

In some cases, the financing party will hire a general engineer, a so-called "bank's engineer," to protect their interests by overseeing quality and certifying that the progress being made is consistent with the amounts of money being drawn by the customer. Typically, they do not become very involved, but sure can be a nuisance to your customer, using them to gain the information they need to satisfy the banks. I usually did not encounter difficulty with these engineers. My advice is to be open and very honest with them and avoid getting between the bank and their engineer as an advocate for or against your customer.

My advice is to prepare for the worst and not underestimate any owner's potential to use or abuse the contract to its advantage. This preparation starts with the cost estimate and development of the contract terms and should be considered in such matters as your project staffing.

I can relate many stories about customers who treated the contract as a "guideline" to be taken advantage of. Most (but not all) of these were in the international arena, where their actions were consistent with local business practice. Most of my domestic experience was under conditions of a buyer's market, with customers who knew that we depended on future sales to them; some of these customers would abuse the contracts. They would raise disputes, assuming that we would ultimately give in, in favor of a future sale. These sales were not guaranteed and often were lost under very competitive bidding. These latter cases were confirmation of the phrase "there is no equity," particularly with aggressive and abusive customers. Be careful and don't be afraid to stand firm when the contract supports your position.

In chapter 7, I will tell the story of a minister in a foreign country who, at the televised contract-signing ceremony, thanked our company and myself, the project manager, for agreeing to build, staff, and equip a training facility, a task which was not at all included in our contracted scope of supply. Like the minister, so many customers in developing countries will assume that the rich foreigners will give them whatever they want, even if it is not in the scope contracted for. Most are a good bit more subtle and effective than this minister (who never got his facility).

In closing this chapter, let me touch on a few important topics:

Contract deliverables: Initially, I recommend that at the outset of your project, you conduct a detailed review of the contract documents in order to identify and list all deliverables, which are typically documents and reports, that you owe to others and items that you should receive. This will avoid embarrassing (and possibly costly) omissions.

Reports: Most contracts will require that you make regular reports addressing progress and commenting on a variety of topics. The most common mistake is to write these reports by painting a trouble-free picture, usually in an effort to avoid conflicts concerning the customers' issues. Later, if disputes arise, the receiver of these reports will produce them as evidence that all was well. Make your reports accurate, telling it like it is; even if the customer has to grudgingly address his issues. Don't set up a later surprise for your customer or a contradiction for yourself.

Change control: Many project teams go too far in trying to please the customer. This attitude will often cause legitimate contract changes to be missed. When the team and project manager believe that the customer has asked for a scope change, the customer should be professionally notified in a timely manner. I do not recommend that the work be done until agreement is achieved, unless the contract terms require that the work proceed under dispute, in which case you should document your position. Often, customers will reject the change notice on principle, sometimes fearing that approval will open the door to many more changes. When the change is legitimate, it is better to be working under dispute than to not raise the issue or to raise it too late. Contracts often have time limits during which you must raise any issue.

Claim management: As with routine changes, it is important to notify the customer of a claim in a timely manner, even when the impacts are not fully determined. I have seen many cases where sellers decide that they are in a serious loss position late in the contract and decide to give notice and develop a claim at that time. Not only is it more difficult to construct a legitimate claim after the fact, but there will be a question of credibility from the owner or third parties involved in the resolution.

Warranties: In most contracts, the warranty terms are well defined, but there may not be a definition of the processes to be followed by the parties. These processes must be defined and agreed to by the parties. They should define how defects are identified, reviewed by your team, and approved as legitimate defects; list requirements for access to the work to repair defects; and finally specify how to determine that the defect has been corrected.

I recommend that you carefully understand your obligations with regard to the extent of warranties on work that was repaired under the basic warranty. Most customers will seek warranties that are evergreen, that is, the obligation to correct defects goes on forever after the correction of an initial defect. These customers will seek to have you maintain a continuing maintenance program. This can be very expensive and is not always provided for in the contract terms.

In chapter 6, I will address the closeout of the contract, which includes establishment of the warranty program. I see it as worth repeating.

CHAPTER 5.

SUBCONTRACT ADMINISTRATION AND SUBCONTRACTOR MANAGEMENT

Contractors in General

Let me begin with some thoughts on subcontractors in general. Since I basically look at my glass as half empty, I see even the best contractors, and there are some very good ones, as a team whose first objective is to make money. By nature, they are not benevolent, and when in trouble, they will find a way to at least break even, even if the truth has to be stretched. Smaller contractors faced with large losses and possible extinction will do whatever they can with claims and even default. Larger contractors employ legal staffs and maintain long menus containing questionable ways to recover losses.

My experience is that when bidding work, most subcontractors will seek to be more competitive by assuming that they will be able to raise the price by at least 10 percent during execution by using overpriced or inappropriate changes. This seemed to be the norm that their employees were expected to achieve. It was so accepted that when we used a contractor's bid in our cost forecasting, we would usually include a provision (or at least identify a risk) to cover it.

I recommend that you be very cautious when considering potential subcontractors who have structures involving multiple entities.

Sometimes, however, this is necessary in order to ensure the necessary skills are assembled.

I would normally avoid awarding a bid to a contractor who would award the bulk of the work to a single sub-tier contractor. Why give up the additional markup and the direct control of the work?

Beware that many good contractors employ contract employees who do not know the companies culture and who will often act at your expense, being short timers anxious to impress their management or because that is the way their prior company did it.

I would also think very carefully about partnerships and joint ventures, especially when they are new or formed specifically for your project. Relationships can quickly fall apart under the stress of execution. I have seen greed and egos result in disputes over whom should be the chief, and when there is a failure to carefully divide the scope, the team becomes dysfunctional. Chapter 9 discusses some of my experience with sharing scope and forming partnerships.

Characteristically, my bottom line is that even the most skilled and conscientious subcontractors are not your partners; they will seek to maximize their share of the profit available on the project. Having this position, I advise that you carefully research the prior performance of any contractor that you put on your bid list. Beyond their work performance, talk to their prior customers to see if they exhibited the predatory attitudes I discussed. Frankly, I must admit that I have made the mistake that I just cautioned you about. In fact, my mistake was worse because my company was the one who had had the bad experience in the past. My reliance on my personal relationships with the contractor's staff cost me embarrassment and brought my credibility into question.

Most large contractors have boilerplate terms and programs addressing their quality and safety programs, designed primarily to meet buyers' demand for these programs. Be cautious. Look into previous contracts to determine the extent to which these paper programs were applied. I urge that you include provisions for your team to inspect both the work and safety of the work and audit the effectiveness of these programs.

Include provisions for the timing of the contractor's responses and corrective actions, including a provision for penalties.

Finally, as I stress in the next chapter, you should look at the safety record of any contractors being considered. Contact their references and assess their quantified safety record.

The Contract Is Critical

Effective subcontractor management begins with writing the contract. I said, "contract," not some standard purchasing agreement. Recently, a friend jokingly told me that she had "hired" her husband to paint her new kitchen. Knowing both people, I was not fully joking when I cautioned her to put a completion clause, with penalties, in her contract. If your selected contractor argues that you do not need a formal contract, you should walk away.

Here again, I will not list all of the necessary terms and conditions, but I will highlight a few issues related to my best lessons learned. Begin with the scope. My advice is to never work with a concept. Take the time to detail the scope, and always make the scope as detailed with any subcontractor as it is with your customer. Pass through the applicable portion of your customer's scope definition and terms, if necessary.

On the subject of pass through, I strongly advise that you review your contract with your customer and formally pass through to the subcontractor any scope, specific issue, or general term that could apply to your subcontractor. Insist on it. This applies to scope, schedule, quality, performance, and administrative requirements, such as reports (including progress photos, schedule development, and personnel matters). The only exception would be the amount (but not timing) of any delay penalties from the prime contract. With a smaller scope, subcontractors cannot be expected to back up the full penalties, even if their performance causes full penalties to be levied.

Be careful with the scope as well. As I said, avoid contracting for an unreasonable schedule in order to build float against the prime contract schedule. Remember that you and the other contributors will have to support the schedule you have subcontracted for. Stick with your original schedule plan.

In the case of subcontracts involving procurements, I strongly endorse passing through the warranty terms in value and in exact timing. Vendors will seek to tie warranties to ex-factory dates, leaving you with a void because your terms will probably tie to your contract completion. This applies to your direct procurements as well.

There are other important terms that I would like to highlight. Payment terms have risks. First, in order to not pay for negative cash flow, align your sub's payment terms with the terms in the prime contract. Next, be sure that payments are not excessively front end loaded and are tied to either very clear progress milestones or easily measurable progress and certainly not elapsed time. Hold some amounts for correction of any punch list items (even the owner's punch list).

Completion terms are also very important. For example, in construction, there should be provisions for a joint walk through, punch list completion timing, careful documentation of "as built" conditions and tests performed, and the like. Like your direct procurements, equipment provided by the sub should have provision for factory progress reviews and quality visits, observation of any critical manufacturing points or tests, as well as documentation of final inspections and tests.

Change control must be defined, as should provision for continuance of the work in the event of a dispute. The broad dispute resolution procedure must be clear and support your ability to meet the prime contract schedule.

I recommend that you think through what correspondence control and reports you want and what requirements you will have for regular meetings, even beyond what you will need to meet your customer obligations. These tools can be valuable in both identifying potential claims and defending them.

In many cases, particularly construction contracts, I recommend that your terms support control of the staff assigned by the contractor.

How Much Oversight?

My story about turning a very large project around to profitability with additional staff is worth repeating. Construction activity on this extended scope project had been overseen by a few field people.. They were overseeing a construction subcontractor that was getting very rich. The subcontractor was doing everything but opening the safe and walking off with my company's money. There were abuses in material control, definition of the quantities that were supposedly installed, and definition of work that was called a scope change. The solution was to spend some money and bring in some experienced construction staff, quantity surveyors, and contract administrators. That was my introduction to the value of subcontractor oversight.

I generally am more comfortable with more specialized oversight. Technical staff, contract administrators, and quality, document control, and safety specialists are all important. There are, however, two problems to be avoided. First, don't let the overseers become exclusively "judges." Their role, a difficult one, is to balance demanding oversight with the ability to help and contribute, a "social worker," so to speak. I say "difficult," because it is not easy to help without becoming part of the problem or providing the contractor with a basis for a claim by leading the contractor into deeper trouble.

The second issue involves staff that must balance an oversight role with direct responsibilities to you in support of the project. An example might be an engineer who oversees work but who must respond to a contractor's inquiries and provide timely information. A document control specialist must ensure that configuration control is maintained for your team and must oversee the contractor's document control. I recommend simply making sure that the individuals understand the differences within their dual roles.

In the prior chapter, I dwelt on the matters of correspondence control and claim avoidance sensitivity. Certainly they are well worth repeating. In my mind, one of the most prevalent failures among your project and construction site teams is their insensitivity to the potential for a contractor's claim or the evidence that a claim is being considered. Perhaps this is because of the closer relationships in the construction environment. The solution is in continual training, strict procedures for communications, and the assignment of staff trained in the administration of contracts.

Bad management of correspondence is also more prevalent at construction sites. I have at times been forced to assign a special reviewer to a site to both get the attention of our staff and ensure that the correspondence was professional and contractually correct. Alternatively, I have demanded that correspondence come to headquarters before issue or that only a site leader that I particularly trusted do the reviews.

Contract Default and Termination

From my point of view, the biggest issue with subcontracting is the potential for a default or termination of the contract by the subcontractor or by you.

While I have had many occasions where terminating a subcontractor would have been appropriate and legally allowable, I have never done so with positive results. There will always be a complex claim and counterclaim situation, with disputes over the costs of completing the work the subcontractor is responsible for and over what are usually fallacious claims from a desperate contractor. In every case of termination, there has been a serious impact on the project schedule, which is usually impossible to recover from.

Default by a subcontractor will be almost as bad in terms of the impact on the project. Having learned about defaults the hard way, I would advise avoiding the situation if at all possible. Avoid this problem by carefully selecting and contracting with your sub. If a default situation then arises, I advise overcoming your emotions and doing everything possible to avoid it. This includes steps like sharing some scope and negotiating the involvement of a second contractor.

CHAPTER 6.

OTHER KEY TOPICS AND LESSONS FOR PROJECT MANAGERS

Do Engineers Really Tinker? Are They Ever Satisfied with Their Work?

A respected colleague and engineering manager once told me that all engineers cannot help but to "tinker" with the designs, even after the designs are issued.

I discussed in the section on subcontract administration the concepts of change avoidance and, when necessary, change management. If your project involves design or detailed engineering as part of your scope of supply, it is imperative that you understand the noble instinct of the engineer or designer to do it the best way possible, even when it is a "redo" or to ignore the cost impact. Sometimes, this noble instinct will cause you to build something that is far more costly than what is required by the scope of your contract and your obligation to the various elements of quality and aesthetics. At other times, revisions to the design may require that your project team amend something already procured; redesign an interfacing contract deliverable, such as the control system, an instrument, or piece of equipment; or at worst rebuild or remanufacture the item. In any case, there is the cost of changing deliverable documents, changing specifications, changing commissioning documents, changing customer manuals, negotiating changes with subcontractors, and so on. There is also the risk of confusion and delay in the construction, in the commissioning, and then in the completion of the contract.

Engineering on a large design and build contract would cost in the range of 5 to 10 percent of the overall contract. I have seen on many occasions that due to the engineer's failure to design to the Original Cost Estimate and level of quality or the engineer's unnecessary revision of the design, the cost of construction, manufacturing, or procurement increased by several times the value of the engineering involved. In some contract types, the cost of the engineering would also increase substantially.

My advice to all project teams is to do everything possible to avoid changes to completed and issued designs. Since engineers inevitably tinker, the project team should be given the opportunity to reject changes, unless the engineering team demonstrates clearly that the change is required to "meet its as-sold objective" or that the contract specification will not be met. I have managed projects for companies where the engineering department dominates, and believe me, changes for actual or perceived improvements can be the fiscal (and often schedule) death of a project.

Control of changes can be improved with the use of some sort of a design freeze. Conducting reviews of the design at various stages and freezing the design at that point will support this technique. Another approach is to insert a review of each revision to designs or specifications issued by the engineering organization by a non-engineering project team member before the revisions reach the constructor or the procurement staff. A third approach is to simply make the change process so difficult for engineering that they simply will not bother. This approach is risky, because legitimate and necessary changes could be missed.

I would also caution against placing too much pressure, penalties or incentives for progress on the engineers. This can often result in the issuance of drawings and specifications that are incomplete or were done for a similar (but not identical) project by an engineer who knows full well that a revision will be necessary.

Engineering can also have a very serious negative impact on a project by adding to the design more than what is required. At one point in every project, there is a cost estimate made to support a bid. That cost estimate is based on an assumed level of quality and a measured set of quantities of all materials. It is natural for an engineer or designer to add strength, numbers, redundancy, and higher quality than is assumed. This is particularly true when the engineer has no direct schedule or fiscal responsibility for the design. This behavior is sometimes driven by an interest in protecting one's professional status. A little overdesign or redundancy will go a long way toward ensuring that there is never a criticism for failure. Whenever I walked through a construction site or new power plant, I could usually identify whether the engineering group or company had a risk in the final construction cost or not. Although I do know one that did not, most companies combining engineering and construction scopes train and sometimes incentivize their engineering staffs to design to specification and code without overdesign. Standalone engineers have no incentive to do so.

One solution is to share the cost risk with the engineering company or provide an incentive to the engineering company to design to the quantities used in the cost estimate. The incentive would be part of the compensation package for the engineering company. This requires a count of the as-designed quantities before releasing the drawings to the field. It can also be effective to have this check of designed quantities done by the engineering and project teams and comparisons made with the quantities assumed in your bid. There will, of course, be variances, but the goal is to have the pluses and minuses offset.

Another technique to control the cost of what is being designed for construction or procurement is to combine the engineering and construction under a single subcontract, should the contract and internal conditions allow. This will place more pressure on the engineers and their management to restrain the natural instincts to overdesign.

In closing on this topic, let me clarify that engineering and procuring material and equipment against specifications prepared by the engineers is an iterative process. Usually the purchase document requires that any of the vendor's exceptions to the specification and their final drawings of the product be approved by the engineers. In the other direction, engineers must wait for drawings from the vendor to complete their (usually more detailed) drawings. Product dimensions, control functions, and operating characteristics are good examples of what the engineers need. I will address this risk again in the section on managers of projects.

These iterations, if not properly managed, will present significant delays in schedule and resultant project cost. Delays by the engineers or unnecessary, incomplete, or vague comments can impact the vendors, manufacturers, and construction contractors. There are several keys to addressing these risks. One key is organizational. I would always advise combining engineering and procurement whenever possible. This approach will also discourage overdesign. The design, supply, and fabrication of engineered piping and pipe hangers are a good example of where design/engineering and supply can be effectively combined. The development of the systems control functions, control logic and software, and supply of control hardware, where needed, is another strong example.

Another key is to provide for expedited communications between the parties. This may require special expediting, routine meetings, or even placing individuals from one organization in the offices of another. The inevitable differences in motive or judgment must be resolved quickly. When there is delay, pride becomes a factor. Frequent exchange of status is important, and finally, the use of non-claim-oriented contractors is a must. In this environment, claims are easily made.

Whose Side Are the Purchasing Agents Really On?

More often than not, a project requires the procurement of material or engineered equipment beyond the basic product that is sold by the company managing the project.

When the project team is required to procure project-specific material or equipment, that task is usually assigned to the company's purchasing department; in some cases, the task is subcontracted. This is where problems might arise. Typically, these organizations are measured by the extent to which they can buy the items for less than a preset target.

I have concluded that almost anyone can buy anything at a lower price if they have freedom to buy from anyone or anywhere they choose, with terms of sale more favorable to the seller, with less favorable warranty terms, by not supporting the project schedule, or by allowing shipment unassembled, untested, or some other "un." Your job and that of your team is to make absolutely sure that you retain approval rights for who, where, exactly what, and under what terms your items are supplied.

The best way to start is to provide price targets, allowing for some inevitable growth during the procurement cycle. For key components, agree with the purchasing staff on which will be the allowable vendors will be (avoid procuring items from areas of the world noted for poor quality). Follow this with a must schedule, considering penalties in some form if the items are not delivered on time. Technical definitions and specifications for the product are important. Performance specifications should be reviewed carefully and checked for conflicts with the detailed specific general or technical terms of the prime contract. Without a good order of precedence among the terms, a vendor could take full advantage of the least demanding terms. Functional requirements alone will most often lead to disputes.

Specify any interim approval or inspection requirements you want to apply, as well as any pre-delivery tests or inspections and the degree to which you want your team or engineers to participate in the tests or inspections.

Consider the labor situation at the location where the purchased item is to be delivered for integration into the project. I have been confronted with laborers that would not handle a component that was fabricated by a nonunion vendor. Here again, your increased cost will be the solution.

Pay particular attention to the warranty terms. I have often been faced with a vendor's warranty that was inconsistent, in duration or the vendor's remedy, with my obligations to my customer. Unfortunately, more money was the answer in the end.

Make it clear what condition the items must be in at delivery. You do not want to be surprised to find you have to pay for any assembly required; it will probably be at a higher rate than the factory cost would have been. This is certain if your subcontractor has you captive or you have to retain technical assistance from the vendor for the assembly.

Remember that your customer specifications must be passed through to your vendor. These customer terms and specifications must be included in the terms of sale for all procurements on the project.

I advise that you arrange for your team to work with the procurement staff to develop a standard set of project-specific terms of purchase, both general and technical. Make sure that all parties agree on these terms, and arrange to have your team review and approve any and all deviations before the order is placed.

Trust me, I have been burned repeatedly by purchasing agents who will "give away" these terms and specifications to optimize price at my net expense or who would do anything to keep the project team, with its detail and approvals, in the dark.

Finally, beware of this problem, which affects many (but certainly not all) purchasing agents. Some agents develop relationships with vendors that are not healthy or even ethical. Gifts of tickets to a ball game, dinner with the spouse, a bottle of their favorite libation, and the like will introduce perceived obligations to the giving vendor or subcontractor. It is more of an issue than you might think. I looked at all bid evaluation documents, and I wanted the team to look at all contract or purchase order changes, just to keep everyone out of trouble.

Your procurement staff must be willing to pursue remedies for the benefit of your project from the suppliers whenever there is a failure to perform to the terms of the specifications. I have encountered situations wherein the purchasing agents will settle on a remedy that provides benefit to a future project, usually in the form of a price concession. This approach will distort the future bidding process in the vendor's favor and will make the agent look good, all at the expense of your project.

Integrating the Logistics Plan with the Procurement Process

Part of this process will be to develop a plan for logistics, which must be integrated into the procurement requirements and the plans at the destination for handling, storage, and receipt inspections. This plan may require retaining specialists to study shipping routes and special equipment requirements for handling, particularly for large or heavy items. Some items will have special requirements for special care during shipping and while in storage, waiting to be used.

The plan must optimize the shipping methods to determine whether vendors should ship to the project location or to a staging site for consolidation with items from other vendors. This latter approach is effective when the project is in a very remote location or overseas. Cost of the various options is a strong consideration. The plan should consider the handling, storage, and care capabilities at the destination. It should also specify when ownership transfers, who pays for care custody and control before use, and who provides the insurance during shipment and when in storage at the destination.

The logistics plan may require using suppliers who are local to a remote or international location. Local sourcing is an advantage in areas where the product quality available is acceptable to both you and your customer. This approach can be cost effective and can avoid customs issues, making it even more favorable. On the other hand, many customers, particularly international customers, will object, favoring specific suppliers or foreign suppliers in general.

In the next chapter, I will speak to the importance of having the proper process at the destination for receiving accountability, inspection for damage, shortage of the items, and formal turnover to the customer (or whoever will have the responsibility for storage and care). I will strongly recommend that the project team have a trustworthy member at the destination with responsibility to account at receiving, participate in the counts and inspections, inform your team of shortage or damage, and supervise the turnover to the party who will store or install the item(s).

Do Your Team Members Understand Their Responsibilities and Limits of Their Authority?

In many cases, you, the project manager, might be the entire team, a very normal situation. In fact, that is the way most sales engineers and salespeople would like to estimate the cost for the bid/proposal, for even the larger projects.

At the other extreme, you may have a team of two-dozen, depending on the size, risk, location, structure, and extent of subcontracting that you decide upon. In the later chapter for managers of projects, I stress the value of staffing projects, in a matrix basis, using staff from functional units where they are trained and from which they are given performance oversight. Combining this matrix approach with a complete set of procedures can go a long way toward ensuring the staff understands their generic jobs and their authorities. I say, "can go a long way," because they will not help unless the functional managers provide the procedures and effective oversight, and because every project has unique scope requirements and contract terms.

Inexperienced project managers will see the matrix as an infringement on their authority. On the other hand, those with experience have learned that there is real value in not having to train and reinvent the procedures/processes and authority definitions project after project. Managers of project managers must be able to assume that the projects will all be run and reported on in the same manner.

As I say later in this chapter, I believe it is necessary to supplement the staff from the matrix with a very thorough project kickoff meeting, wherein the project-specific scope and terms are reviewed, along with several other topics I will discuss later.

My biggest problems in this regard were with the managers hired to supervise the operations at a construction site or other remote location. These people were there, in most cases, because they were willing to be away from home in exchange for the independence they perceived that they would have. Most of these individuals were strong technically, having "grown up" doing field work. They generally had good people skills. On the other hand, they were not strong contractually, administratively, or in a business management sense. For the most part, they were most interested in doing things their way and maintaining their independence (which is why they went to the field). Your response must be to use people trained in the matrix whenever possible and to be there at the site (or have your functional managers be there), often walking and talking to everyone to understand what is really going on.

The bottom line is that a successful project team will be made up of good, well-trained people working to standard processes, knowing what to do and what to expect from others on the team, and knowing that they will be rewarded for the success of the team as a whole.

What Relationship Do You Want with Your Customer?

While I always worked very hard to maintain a constructive relationship with my customers, there were a few that I wanted to fire. I am sure that there were a few that wanted to fire me, usually because I had a nasty habit of reading the contract.

To avoid these firings, there are a few tips that will help you establish a strong and professional relationship with key customer people and third-party staff assigned on the project.

As I address your relationship with your customer, you can apply this guidance to your relationships with any third-party counterparts representing the customer or other entities, such as a bank.

In the majority of cases, the customer will be fair, will want you to be likewise, and will want the project to be successful. Most individuals assigned by your customer to oversee the project realize that if you and your project team are successful, they will be seen as successful also. If the project fails to meet expectations, these individuals will be considered less than fully successful within their companies. Therefore, these people will normally work with the project managers to ensure success of the project.

I say "normally," because there will be exceptions that you must be prepared to deal with. Typically, these exceptions have the idea that their path to success is to make you and your project staff look bad. This can be an individual trait or can reflect the culture of your customer's company. Being prepared is key, particularly in the early stages of the project, when the customer's approach is yet to be determined.

I have seen good managers fail because they become obsessed with winning against their troublesome customer counterparts or other overseers. No matter how troublesome your counterparts are, work with them and at the same time build what relationship you can with the senior people in the customer's organization. In this situation, try to find ways to involve more senior individuals in the customer's organization in project matters and meetings, but never openly criticize or have open conflict with your direct counterpart.

On rare occasions, customers may have motives contrary to yours. Some will seek to take advantage of your interest in being fair and keeping them satisfied. Others will do the same from a cultural base. I have had an occasion or two where I was convinced that the customer had changed its interest and did not want the project. Once while building a small project in an international location controlled by "very bad guys," the customer seemed to do everything possible to discourage our interest, to delay our progress, and later to cause the equipment to not perform. I concluded that they were hoping that we would default, terminating the project, their cost would be recovered and they would not have to work among the bad guys.

Frankly, a laid-back customer can also be dangerous. I always valued a customer who was aware, knowledgeable, and in my face. This seemed to keep me more alert and focused. Further, that type of customer often had good ideas or insights that I was never too proud to use.

Good communications are most important. I recommend strongly that these communications be both formal and informal and as open as possible. By formal, I mean that, as I said, you should schedule regular meetings with published agendas and recorded proceedings. Your credibility will be enhanced with techniques like maintaining an open action items list, with accountably on both sides. Written communications should be used for formal contract-based notices and requirements. In my chapter on contract administration, I made it clear that I am against informal written or e-mail communications. This applies to the project manager as well. The only use of e-mail that I might support would be for matters like arranging phone calls, meetings, or meeting agendas.

My idea of acceptable informal communications would be regular visits, phone calls, and joint walks of the project areas. These discussions can be established as off the record when you want to explore sensitive matters or when negotiating solutions. In chapter 4, I addressed these communications, stressing that they be minimized and that they be restricted to key individuals, like the project manager or the manager of projects. On the other hand, I would never expose the project to risk based on these informal communications until the key matters are formally agreed to and documented. As with most communications, you will learn more by listening.

Earlier, I discussed customers who operate within different business practices and cultures; I will do so again in the chapter on international projects. The only solution is to understand and have experience with the local business practices and culture. Some customers will try to use the language factor to their advantage. Many will insist on conducting meetings, correspondence, and discussions in their language, sometimes on principle, sometimes pleading a poor capability in your language, and sometimes with the simple objective of gaining an advantage. In the case of capability, don't be fooled. In any case, many will have a good working knowledge of your language and will listen carefully to discussions that you think are private. Sometimes, customers who do understand your language will use a translator, both to buy time to think and to allow for reversals attributable to mistakes by the translator. Be careful in this circumstance. Use a trusted translator on your side when you cannot avoid this circumstance.

When there are valid issues with the customer, directed scope changes, for example, don't be afraid to seek fair changes. Some companies and individuals retain the idea that one should not challenge or offend the customer. I disagree, but I would always be fair with the customer and would expect that the customer be the same. On the other hand, after trying the other steps that I discussed, I have responded to a customer's unfair claims or failure to resolve issues or make changes that I asked for with changes that were questionable, in order to build a basis for a balanced negotiation. In cases where the customer's representatives have interfered, using inappropriate direction in the field, contact with my subs, or direct correspondence, after exhausting other strategies, I have not hesitated to issue notice of intent to claim for cost or schedule impact. This would often cause the practices to stop.

Hopefully, these latter steps are not necessary, and the constructive relationship that I always tried to achieve will exist in your project.

How Do You React to Costs Growing Out of Control?

First, I would stress the importance of communicating openly with your team and your management when there is a potential cost overrun situation. Be open and share the details so that you can focus and be helped in the areas that need cost control assistance. In most companies, there are specialists who can help. The worst thing that you can do is to let pride or fear allow the situation to get worse. Don't fall back on hope or rely on prayer. Recognize that the glass is half empty and will probably drain further. The situation will get worse when there is a big surprise later.

The second basic mistake that I have seen is to react by cutting personnel; you'll need their help to turn the situation around.

Throughout my career and when consulting as an expert witness, I have seen the same mistake over and over. I will relate one very good example in chapter 7. When projects get in trouble and face cost overruns, they often promptly cut the staff that was planned to properly manage the project. As I said, I have proven to myself that this is absolutely the wrong approach. When you consider that the total of the project indirect cost is well under 10 percent of the project total cost, you must realize that you cannot make a big impact on the final cost by reducing a few percentage points of your indirect cost. Actually cutting staff cost will loosen your control on the project activities and the forces that are driving the cost upward. The only cut I would make would be the individual or individuals who clearly caused the problem or covered it up.

My advice is to get some help from people who are not defensive about the cause of the overruns; they can help you find the root causes. Next, believe the indicators, rely on the expertise and experience of others, quickly make an aggressive plan, and add staff if necessary. You should work on your cost tracking system to allow you to track, on a very short-term basis, the effect of your corrective actions. You may have to take direct control of cost-related decisions.

Do You Know Where Your Over-budget Costs Have Gone?

Earlier, I related a story about a senior manager, working in a system where company accountants (and not the project team) maintained both the project ledger and the cost forecasting system, continually asked where the bleeding was. There was no recognition of the fact that the system was totally inadequate and that there was no basis for answering the question.

The question, however, was an excellent one. Only by recognizing the individuals responsible for the cost variances incurred to date and the predicted cost to complete the project can you work with the responsible individuals to stop the bleeding. This can be done by correcting past practices and working to avoid predicted variances in the future.

After fixing the basic cost planning system by placing the cost recording and forecasting responsibility where it belonged, with the project manager and his team, we set out to build a process for tracking the bleeding. Basically, we set up a computer-based system to identify variances to the cost plan. We were to identify variances to cost incurred and variances in predicted future costs against the budget or base cost plan. I hope this sounds familiar.

It was necessary to train all members of the project team to recognize changes in the cost to date and in the future cost relative to the budget. The concept of a commitment to future cost changes was critical. People had to recognize that a contract change or cost actually incurred was not the only thing we wanted to focus on.

The most difficult concepts included recognizing commitments made by the field staff that led to cost variances and commitments to increase staff, along with recognizing design changes by engineers.

We developed a flexible report and approval sheet for use on all cost increase elements. We integrated the reports and approvals with some existing technical approval documents in order to ensure that approvals were given with full awareness of the cost impact and that the cost impacts were assigned to a specific individual or small group. Frankly, in doing so, we identified cases where approvals were being given by individuals who were incapable or possibly conflicted in their interests. I was always concerned with managers approving added staff, engineers approving their design changes, and purchasing agents approving changes from vendors with whom they had questionable relationships.

Rather than discuss each area of control and the need to evaluate and document cost changes, here is a list of examples of when questions should be raised:

When work direction is given to a subcontractor

When a decision is made to add staff, in the home office or in the field

When a vendor contract is awarded for an amount above (or below) the budgeted value

When your productivity measures clearly show an overrun in an area

When vendors or subcontractors are awarded contract changes

When a scope concession is made to the owner

When a design change is issued to a contractor or vendor

I will continue to discuss the importance of transparency and openness with the information on cost overruns or potential overruns (risks). The information should be exposed early in order to get the help you need and to avoid surprises. Be careful; I have encountered senior managers and key financial staff that for usually obvious reasons wanted to keep these problems secret. If the secret was kept the project manager and the team were the ultimate losers when these secrets were ultimately uncovered. Senior managers can at times be conveniently forgetful when the ultimate surprise comes.

To build such a tracking system, we had to first identify every element of cost in the budget and then decided whom the people are who can make decisions in these cost areas. As an additional step, we set out to build in an approval process by these key individuals.

Can You Manage Project Revenues/Sales and Margins?

My message in this section applies to both project managers and their managers.

I will not attempt a discussion of generally accepted accounting practices but will highlight a few basic principles that I learned to manage projects by. Over and over again, I have seen teams inappropriately overstate sales/revenue or margin only to be required to reverse these incorrect bookings in future periods, bringing sometimes very serious personal and corporate consequences. Let me explain.

The projects that we are using as the basis of the experiences and lessons in this book typically last over multiple fiscal periods; that is, months, quarters, or annual fiscal periods. In this situation, it is tempting to use the partially completed projects to inappropriately fill voids in or defer revenue or margins being booked by the company or associated profit center during the interim fiscal periods.

First, to avoid these mistakes, I recommend that project managers fully understand the accounting practices and procedures used by their company, and further, project managers must be aware of what the company is doing with regard to booking sales/revenue and cost as well as the resultant margins. Next understand that achieving an otherwise missed company fiscal goal is one motive for overbooking at the company level. Satisfying this motive could ensure that project teams or others are awarded bonuses associated with this "achievement." Don't be tempted and let others misrepresent the current situation on your project in order to best serve their performance measures or other objectives. It is you who will be held accountable for any mistake.

Earlier, I admonished project managers to avoid any kind of surprises, good or bad. Reversals in revenue or margin previously taken are one such surprise, a bad one. On the other hand, I have often seen project staffs think they will be doing the company a big favor by overstating cost to complete forecasts or holding recognized revenues down and planning on a big "atta boy (or girl)" later. This theoretically good late surprise can in some cases cause the company to fail to meet its fiscal plans or act unnecessarily to cut costs, even jobs, during the interim periods. I have seen these mistakes happen more than once.

The message is, no matter what the pressures brought to bear or the personal motives, the project teams and company financial teams must follow a few basic guidelines.

First, revenue booked to the company ledger must be related to the project's true earned value, which should be accurately determined as discussed earlier. In the case of revenue earned for equipment sold as part of the project, the most correct method I have seen used is to book the revenue when the equipment is complete and shipped, not till them. Relating the revenue booked to the percentage of planned cost incurred (or in some way to the schedule achieved) is a common mistake used by teams in trouble in order to mask the trouble or satisfy the company appetites for financial results. Don't go there.

The second guideline relates to not comparing the cost incurred to date to the value of the work completed or to not maintaining an accurate cost at completion forecast, which can be compared with the cost provided in the total cost of sales/revenue used in making interim entries in the company books. The method of developing and maintaining an accurate cost at completion forecast has been discussed, along with the common motives for not doing so. Managing this forecast falsely, for whatever motive, is the most common error of commission, and the one with the most serious consequences, that I have seen in the project business.

Finally, surprises can be avoided by maintaining a strong ledger of potential cost risks and opportunities, as discussed in chapter 3. Every project has, almost by definition, a number of cost risks, which a competent team will identify. As I said, the only variable will be the probability, which is a judgment to be made honestly by the team. Cost saving opportunities do generally occur and, as with cost risks, can be measured or consolidated with risks using honestly determined probabilities.

In order to avoid over- or under-booking the sales/revenue at any point in time, the team must consider the future impact of the cost risks and opportunities. The key is the judgment used in consolidating these factors with their costs and probabilities. This honest consolidation of potential cost impacts is part of the true cost at completion forecast, the most commonly abused process in a project team's management of variances.

In summary, unless a project team has a basic understanding of the accounting principles involved, has the systems in place to measure earned value and maintain an accurate forecast of cost at completion, has the integrity to tell the truth they know, and has the strength to say no when other interests seek to change or ignore the facts, there will be unwanted surprises (and usually very serious consequences) for the project and the company. Somehow, it is always the project team and manager who are blamed when unpleasant surprises arise.

How Well Do You Track Your Claims and Counterclaims?

In chapters 4 and 5 and earlier in this chapter, I discussed the contractual relationships with your customer and your subcontractors. I encourage formalized change control; do not be afraid to professionally put changes forward in a timely manner, even to the customer. For various reasons, many project managers are unwilling to put changes forward to their customer; I suppose that they want to avoid a distasteful situation, hoping for the opportunity later. In fact, most standard terms for projects provide a fixed time period during which notice must be given of an intent to submit a claim.

What I would like to stress here is the importance of understanding the contract terms relative to submission and resolution of claims. It is important to carefully track and make visible to all parties any notices of intent to claim or unresolved claims and counterclaims. I would insist that your contractors be required, in their regular reports, to identify all notices, open claims, and even claims being contemplated. In a similar manner, I would insist that your team use your reports to your customer in the same manner. Remember, surprises are bad, and in most cases, relationships don't get better, in fact, they usually get worse as the project goes on, making resolution more difficult later. I said earlier, when I felt that claims identified by the owner or subcontractor were fallacious, I would not hesitate to identify even marginal counterclaims in an effort to build some form of offset. Note that the condition for doing this was an objective judgment on your part that the claims against you were fallacious. Maintain an active data base with all correspondence and documentation related to all claims and counterclaims.

How Do You Ensure Quality from Vendors or During Installation/ Construction?

The extent to which your team should oversee the quality built into software, material, equipment provided, and the construction is purely based on experience and judgment. You can hope for the best, but I do not advise it, having been taken advantage of many times. Like any risk, you should consider the relative negative impact of the particular element of quality, your experience with the provider, and your capabilities to effectively oversee the activity.

Early in my career, on a project to build a large containment vessel, we decided to over-inspect radiographs of 10 percent of the welds and only expand our inspections if more than a set percentage of the welds failed and had to be repaired. Having a requirement for no defects, this approach was just plain silly. If we found defects within a 10 percent sample, surely there were defects requiring repair in the other 90 percent. Expanding our sample size would not lead to a different conclusion. We stopped all work and checked the radiographs on all welds and made many repairs, a very expensive process.

Later in the construction of the vessel, we found that most of the attachments to the vessel did not meet the specifications for the material being used. The vendor had provided certifications that were obviously false. Here again, we either hoped or trusted and did not sample the material being certified. These two mistakes were very costly in time and dollars but were good learning experiences.

You cannot over check everything; start with classifying work supplied or performed into levels of criticality. We called it levels of essentiality. Essentiality is determined by the cost or schedule impacts encountered in the event that quality issues went undetected. The next broad step is to ensure that you deal with suppliers and contractors who have real, not merely paper-based, quality plans. Start your plan by ensuring that the supplier/contractor is following its plan in the essential areas.

For suppliers of essential elements, ensure that your terms of purchase provide for notice to you of critical inspections, tests, and shipment dates and allow you access to the shop for oversight and pre-shipment inspections. Just knowing that you might be coming might motivate your supplier to improve their quality control. Check the packaging as well, particularly for international shipments.

Do the same for contractors. Ensure that they have an adequate plan and follow it. Don't allow them to assume that you are responsible for basic quality assurance. You are first the over checker, ensuring that the subcontractor or vendor implements their own plan and sees that their inspections and checks are being done properly. Next you should pick highly essential items for your overcheck sampling. If defects are found, don't accept the explanation that you found an unusual situation. Look further. For larger integrated systems, insist that the contractor provide you with a system completion record before accepting the system for further testing. The contractor should provide, for example, material certifications, weld records, equipment alignment data, electrical system test data, hydrostatic test data, and a record of a final walk-through inspection, which your project team should participate in.

For essential items, consider that sabotage is a possibility. I have seen many cases of rags and other debris being left in closed vessels, piping, electrical enclosures, or equipment, none of which could be attributed to carelessness or the infamous rodent. Your team should participate in final pre use inspections.

Finally, do not assign quality as a secondary task to a staff member. In most cases, you will pay more than a proper effort will cost.

Why Is It Important to Control Your Documents?

In chapter 4, I discussed the importance of creating and maintaining control of documentation that relates to implementing and defending the contract in a legal sense. In this section, my comments will refer to process documents or deliverables necessary to define the work.

In most cases of a loss of control of your process documents, the inevitable cost impact will be aggravated when there are contractual issues or disputes. When a drawing is revised and does not get to (or is late getting to) the vendor or contractor, there will usually be the cost of rework, the extent of which will vary with the degree of lateness. Vendors and contractors will often use the lateness as an excuse for their delays. They will often overstate the cost impacts in a way that is difficult to dispute. Holdups or oversights at any of a multitude of activity interface points will therefore cause a cost impact.

Similarly, late specifications, late comments, or late approvals of vendor or contractor documents, procedures, or instruction manuals can have serious impacts. Only good procedures, clear responsibility and oversight or measurements will minimize the impact of the inevitable claims that arise.

On a large project, I advise assigning (or sharing the assignment of) a trained project administrator to handle all documents. Most team members are not interested in documents and often put them low on their priority list. If there is a substantial physical distance between the parties, I recommend investing in the equipment necessary to transmit the drawings, specifications, or other documents electronically and print them locally. No matter how it is transmitted, you must ensure that there is a process of dated and written acceptance by the receiving party, the vendor, the subcontractor, or other party.

On the other hand, don't let the speed and ease of documents produced electronically lead to unnecessary revisions. Remember the lawyer who wants to count revisions and changes, without looking at the realistic impact of the changes. Finally, let me remind you that one of the main causes for claims by vendors or contractors is the use of outdated documents. I assure you that the cost of the rework involved will be overstated.

In the chapter on contract management, I addressed the importance of indexing and controlling the various correspondences that must be stored for retrieval. When negotiating settlements, pursuing or defending claims, or acting as an expert witness, I have repeatedly seen the value of complete and good documentation that is easy to access.

How Is the Project Best Kicked Off?

I strongly recommend beginning each project by reading your contract, in all of its sometimes boring and always legalistic detail. Your entire team should do so. I have suggested acknowledging this with their signatures. Time after time, I have seen customers be offended, project managers lose basic credibility, and unnecessary costs be incurred because the contract stayed on the shelf until the team was in trouble.

In chapter 3, while discussing the plan for controlling the scope of supply under your contract, I made reference to the value of kickoff meetings with the proposal and sales staffs and then with your customer. At that time, I promised more detail about this meeting. I recommend developing a menu of steps for the project kickoff, including the standard formal agenda for these kickoff meetings. Beyond being the starting point for your activities, these meetings are a mandatory step with regard to your relationship with your customer. You must know what is *not* in writing and what understanding your customer and your sales staff have of what is in writing.

At the first meeting, the marketing and sales team should hand all documentation to the project management team. The documentation begins with the customer's initial inquiry and the contract, and includes any changes or supplementary agreements. There should be copies of all documented meetings and negotiation notes, and of course a copy of the Original Cost Estimate and any supplements or revisions. The documentation must include any agreements with potential partners or subcontractors and cost estimates received from them.

As I have said and will repeat, be alert to these supplementary agreements. Sales teams often use such agreements in order to "hide" their agreements from the senior management, who want to know how the negotiations went. The existence of such separate written, oral, or implied commitments of scope or additions or changes should be documented, along with a clear statement of where the scope might be defined other than the scope section of the terms. It is important to document this carefully, as more often than not; your customer will raise the issue of what else they were promised.

At this internal kickoff meeting, you should discuss and document agreements on many topics including, but not limited to, your plans for development of the project schedule, communications procedures and limitations, notices, change procedures, individual responsibilities and limits of authority, planned equipment sources and subcontracting plans, transportation plans, staffing commitments made, expectations for and compliance with all terms and conditions, payment terms, and most importantly the scope of work. This is the time, using these topics as discussion points, to extract from the sales team their knowledge of customer expectations for all elements of the documented scope, as well as their expectations for what is not documented. It is critical to take the time to discuss each element of the scope and functional requirements.

When in doubt about the agenda, simply walk through the entire contract and the pre bid approval documents, questioning or clarifying each item.

Other subjects for the agenda, such as the identified cost risks and opportunities, will be discussed in the chapter on managers of project managers. In closing this meeting, you the project manager should make it clear to the sales staff that they have no further authority to agree to changes in the scope or any other part of the contract. They should maintain their normal relationships with the customer, but they have no project authority and certainly should never be the point of contact between the customer and your company concerning project matters.

In chapter 3, when addressing the need to clarify the scope requirements and expectations, I addressed the need for an early meeting with the customer on the subject. I called this a "customer kickoff" meeting. The standard formal agenda for this meeting should go well beyond clarifications of the scope of your project.

In this meeting, you should also discuss and document agreement on many topics including, but not limited to, your plans for development of the project schedule, the schedule itself, communications procedures and limitations, notices, change procedures, meeting schedules, individual responsibilities and limits of authority, planned equipment sources and subcontracting plans, expectations for and compliance with all terms and conditions, and your staffing plans. This is the time to bring out customer expectations for all elements of the documented scope as well as their expectations for anything that is not documented. It is critical to take the time to discuss each element of the scope, functional requirements, and contract terms.

After completing these steps, the project manager must take the time to communicate the final agreed-to scope of work to the entire team. I have had sad experience with team members who were not fully fluent in the scope, who provided scope that were not intended to be supplied, or who argued that they should not to supply what was required. Cost was incurred unnecessarily, time was lost, and a customer was unnecessarily annoyed.

When Is a Construction Phase Complete?

When a project includes a combination of construction activity and follow-on activity to commission or operate a system or equipment, it is extremely important to ensure that the construction is complete, that the conditions are well documented, and that the organization performing the follow-on work understands and accepts the conditions. Any conditions or process steps that are required by your customer must be included. If you do not ensure that these steps are taken, I can assure you that your team will be caught directly in the middle of a dispute between the two parties.

Begin with the negotiations of the construction contract, including a process whereby the contractor is given a specific list of tests that demonstrate that the civil, mechanical, electrical, and electronic work is complete. The contractor must be required to document the condition of the work, system by system, component by component. This documentation must include a punch list of incomplete work, all test results, all unresolved quality issues, and the results of a system inspection conducted jointly by your team, the contractor, and the party who is accepting the system for further work. This documentation package must also include a copy of the as-built drawings and specifications for the system or component involved.

Once the systems are complete, the inspections are done, and the documentation (ideally certified by the constructor) is submitted and approved by your team, the follow-on work can start. As I said earlier, it is important that the party doing the follow-on work be a party to accepting the systems. At that point, the construction is complete, except for the punch list documented for each system. This documentation will be needed when it comes time for your team to hand over the completed project to your customer. For this reason, it is a good idea to include your customer in these inspections.

At this point, a caution is in order. Often I have seen a project team rush to this point, when the system is not truly complete. This was usually driven by a desire to avoid completion penalties. The result was an excessively long punch list that the contractor had to complete later, with the system under the control of the follow-on party or the customer after preliminary acceptance of the overall work. The contractor may ultimately be required to remobilize. My experience is that this approach usually results in extra delay and disputes among the parties about access to the work to complete the details. Finish the work before attempting to test or use the work.

What to Think About When Approaching the End: Warranties?

As you approach completion of the project, I advise that you carefully review the terms of your contract concerning warranties and the overall steps in acceptance by the owner. Often there are differing milestones and differing definitions of any one milestone. As a milestone, mechanical completion, for example, can have many differing definitions. These milestones can be linked to performance or progress penalties and often define limits on the sequence of work to achieve other milestones or the final testing required.

My experience is that sales, legal, and contract development teams typically do not understand the cost impact or time required to satisfy the various alternatives in the project acceptance process. As a result, I have seen processes written into contracts that give the customer all sorts of unreasonable leverage when they wish stretch the process out and have additional scope or operating support.

Shortly after project startup, you should discuss the completion and acceptance process with the customer to ensure there is a mutual understanding of the contract requirements. I have had customers who have tried hard to avoid the completion and acceptance process in order to keep the contract open and have you continue maintenance or operation of the product.

You should ensure that your contractors are aware of the required process and definitions, assuming that these terms have been passed through into their contracts.

The warranty contract provisions should be your next concern. You should work with the customer to put in place a documented process for administering the warranties. This process should be implemented long before completion, overlapping the completion process. I recommend defining the individual contact points, defining who has the authority to agree that an alleged defect is truly a defect under the contract provisions and who has the authority to agree that the matter is corrected. Remember that warranty work can be completed after acceptance of the overall project by your customer; it is important not to mix the warranty work with the punch list for project completion. Alleged defects that show up during initial testing or use should be classified as warranty defects unless they prevent achievement of the performance requirements. The significance is that many customers will insist that these items be corrected as a condition of acceptance of the project rather than later under the warranty terms and procedures. Component failures or system performance shortfalls that do not affect the overall performance specifications can be classified as warranty items.

Another detailed process that is necessary is identifying and clearing so-called punch list or work completion items. There are a few key points to watch out for here. First, there should be agreement on a date by which the lists are developed by the customer. The lists can be delivered on a system-by-system or component-by-component basis but must be submitted by a specified date or milestone. This can be encouraged by having the customer participate in the inspections done at construction completion. Absolutely do not let the lists "dribble in," or you will never get done.

Next, have your team review the lists and accept only what is a true defect, allowing for a negotiated settlement of the rejected items. Make your position clear about what is and is not a true defect. I then recommend seeking agreement with the customer on when each item is to be completed. Use the completion milestones when necessary. It is foolish to delay completion or beneficial use to complete an item that requires an extensive shutdown of the equipment or the systems. The work can often be done under the warranty program during a planned service shutdown later. Finally, establish a master list and share it with the customer. When items are corrected or completed, have the customer sign off on its completion. This is important because there are often differing opinions or short memories within the customer's organization.

If your company has contracts for either ongoing service or hardware/parts, I suggest that you include the responsible individuals in your closeout meetings with the customer. I suggest further that you have a formal turnover to the service people in your company to document what your open warranty or other obligations are. You may want to have your service team implement any remaining warranty obligations. Having a single interface will support the service relationship with the customer and simplify the planning and work implementation.

What Must Be Done to Close the Project?

Having discussed the preparations for the end of the project, I can only stress the importance of completing what you have put in place. You must document acceptance at each of the completion milestone points. It must be documented even if you must negotiate and document a supplementary agreement to cover the resolution of any disputes at any time. The key is to document achievement of the milestones as soon as possible, allowing you to proceed with work for which the milestone is a prerequisite or even stop (or limit) any applicable delay penalties.

I have experienced many cases where the customer wanted to have beneficial use of the equipment or system but was not willing to acknowledge that a completion milestone had been met. Typically, you will have very little leverage should you allow this, so I strongly recommend against it. With beneficial use, your customer has no incentive to accept the milestones and you are at risk of taking on a continuing maintenance role.

What Is Your Responsibility for Safety on the Project?

In a career of project management, most of which included heavy construction, I have had two people lose their lives as a result of construction activity. Although I have had to deal with international conditions where the lack of hard hats (or even shoes) typified the almost nonexistent sensitivity to safety, both of these tragedies occurred domestically. In both cases, however, the individuals died because they did things that were well beyond common sense; even though there were no violations of safety laws or codes, I felt as directly responsible as anyone.

I developed contempt for domestic contractors who presented elaborate safety plans but never really took the responsibility to implement them. These firms could come up with any number of ways to distort their injury and loss of work time statistics. It was appalling. On the other side were international firms who were influenced by cultural pressures and lack of regulation. These cultures made it difficult (but not always impossible) to implement basic safety programs. Some would not implement the basic safety procedures we expected; yet others would agree to use safety equipment that we provided. I can remember watching a large group of women excavate a foundation; they were barefoot, hatless, wearing long saris, and carrying metal disks on their heads. They poured the concrete using the same techniques. I was troubled but could only provide the equipment they needed and strongly encourage its use. The point is that you should feel responsible and do all you can in the interest of safety.

My advice is to have a safety plan for your staff and provide the necessary equipment to implement it. Your staff can be tasked with the obligation to accept or reject the sub contractor's plan and to continuously audit the full implementation.

For subcontractors, I would begin with the selection process. When evaluating the bidders, you should heavily weight their safety records, based on both statistics and comments from others. Once chosen, your contract must detail the subcontractor's obligations. The first requirement should be a plan that your team must approve. Second should be provisions to audit their implementation of their plan. Third, there must be a definition of the manner and timeliness of the contractor's response to your audit findings. As with quality, divide the time of your staff between auditing the contractor's compliance with their own plans and doing direct safety audits in the work areas. Finally, I would advise incorporating some form of penalty if the contractor fails to maintain a satisfactory level of safety measures.

The bottom line is that you must take responsibility for the safety of everyone involved with your project.

CHAPTER 7.

THE "EXCITING" INTERNATIONAL PROJECTS

I have executed or given oversight to projects on every continent that does not end in "-tic" and visited almost all of the projects. In doing so, I have spent about equal time managing domestic and international projects. Along the way, I have developed a few convictions about a few project processes and philosophies that require more attention in the international environment.

There are key differences in the areas of staffing, material control and management, accounting, contract administration, subcontracting, local business practices, procurement, project structure, communications, and the need to be physically present at the international location. I will comment on each of these.

Staffing

In chapter 9, which is intended for managers of project managers, I will discuss various general staffing and project organization strategies. My comments here are intended to highlight the strategies and lessons learned that are relevant to the international environment.

One domestic engineering company that I was with operated in an area where it seemed that the culture was to not have a passport. A trip to a metropolitan area forty miles away was a project in itself. People just did not want to travel. The quick solution for international projects was to go to the marketplace and contract with individuals who wanted to work abroad. There were many individuals and so-called "body shops" available to provide such staffing support. This approach can be attractive, because it is quick and allows for staffing with individual contractors who have international experience and are long over the culture shock that often comes with these assignments.

I soon learned, however, that loyalty, interest in growth with the company, and some familiarity with the company's policies and practices were just as valuable as being comfortable working abroad. With time, I learned that most individual contractors had not been able to gain longevity with a large company or were impatient for a quick buck, pound, rupee or peso, as the case might be. I concluded that when I could not staff with our own employees or contractors I knew well personally or who were from reputable body shops, I would staff with a mixture of employees and contractors. I learned to insist on staffing all the leadership positions and any position dealing with accounting or contract administration with employees from within our company.

One of my most powerful lessons learned came when I became frustrated with our project management and local leaders who had been assigned from our home office. I assigned a company employee who had been working in the subject country on other matters but who understood the culture. I gave him project management and local leadership roles. The individual had very limited project management experience, but he had a local staff and understood the language well. We gave him some technical support. In a country where everyone had a hand out or in your pocket, his contribution was invaluable. His personal comfort locally, his understanding of the culture and its business practices, and his knowledge of the language gained him respect very quickly. His loyalty to our company eliminated many of my concerns. With some support, the ideal combination of local knowledge and company loyalty overcame his lack of project management experience. This was a good lesson, and I went on to apply it over and over.

Finally on this topic, I would like to expand on a point I made earlier. In chapter 6, I advised not responding to cost issues by cutting your staff. I learned this lesson after becoming involved with an international project that was in deep cost trouble. I was given the opportunity to manage the completion of that project as well as a large contract extension. Over the serious cost-oriented objections of my senior management, my first steps were to change our in-country management team and increase the number on that team from five to about twenty. It seemed that the prior project manager had left most site activities to a local contractor and a third-country contracting firm who had a distant relationship with our company. This distant relationship earned the company unwarranted trust with the prior project manager and our senior management.

While we had fixed price contracts, both of these contractors were operating as if their contracts were cost type, not fixed price contracts. Together, they were stealing us blind. They overstated quantities of material installed, agreed to unnecessary scope changes, mistreated equipment, and abused progress payment terms. With the expanded staff of construction experts in all technical disciplines, materials control people, and contract administrators—and a lot of my personal and headquarters staff time on site—we were able to stop these costly abuses and easily overcome the additional cost burden associated with the staff that I had added. We made the contract extension very profitable.

Realistically, I found that doing an occasional large project in the international environment is risky for any company. Work in this environment requires a standing staff of experienced field employees, either in the home office or in the locality where the projects are to be done. This means that there is a higher level of risk for companies that are new to the international environment or only take such contracts on occasion.

If you seek to be successful in the international environment, I recommend not taking the occasional international project. If you do, you must maintain a seed staff of loyal company-trained and internationally experienced people willing to give you continuity on the projects.

Material Control and Management

My learning curve on managing the flow and control of material to installation, fabrication, or construction locations was difficult and steep. It began with my first international project, when we had to replace material and equipment that we thought had been shipped and received but was not; this took more and more time, and we were continually delayed by missing material.

Having passed the statute of limitations, I can now disclose that in this case, my staff and I would routinely take substantial numbers of large hard-covered suitcases of urgently needed parts or supplies into the country, to replace what had been "lost." On all of our frequent visits, we would proceed through customs in this developing country without declaring our cargo in order to avoid the usual extended delays in customs clearance. We were armed with only a little courage and a modest facilitating payment. I finally decided against continuing this practice and assigned trusted staff members to properly receive, account for, and protect the material arriving at international locations.

After joining another large firm, I found task forces from a major national consulting firm studying project materials practices in the project arena. It seems that there was a continuing need to re-procure all sorts of material and equipment that had apparently been bought and shipped to project locations but which had never arrived. The result was a substantial increase in project costs and a delay in their schedules. The problem occurred with all projects but predominantly with the international projects.

There was lots of talk about implementing sophisticated bar code systems and blaming the vendors, packers, and shippers. The primary answer, however, was internal and quite simple. After visiting a site or two, I was appalled by the processes used. It seems that vendors were directed to pack and ship material to export packers, who then loaded the containers for shipment to the project owners or their construction contractors at the construction site. Our project teams seemed to just "wave good-bye."

At many locations, particularly in developing countries, I found the most beautiful fences made of reinforcing bar and homes with top-of-the-line industrial fixtures, pumps, and so on. Yes, the vendors and packers did make mistakes, but the problem was that there was no control and oversight of the receiving, unpacking, and storage processes. The stuff just disappeared or was used in the wrong application. It was not rocket science, nor did it require an assessment by a nationally known consulting firm.

Like in my customs clearance story, the answer was clear. At each project location, we placed a professional material manager, and local staff if necessary, to supervise the unpacking and storage of the material. Our people were required to check the packing lists, count the items unpacked, and report any shortages or damage. A fairly common system of documentation was used for that process. Our staff was then responsible for the security of the equipment and material until it was turned over, with an itemized list and an acceptance signature by the owner or contractor.

Once we got control of what we thought we had sent we needed to avoid surprises when we opened the boxes. As I said earlier, any kind of surprise is unacceptable. Surprises often occurred when a container or box was opened only to find that the quantities were short in count, items were damaged, or items were incorrect. If the items were not unpacked until they were needed for construction or commissioning, there would be a definite and usually costly delay. Having learned this, I insisted that all boxes be opened and the contents inspected and counted upon arrival at the project location. This allowed time for recovery with resupply and also for developing both the necessary insurance claims for shipping damage and documentation necessary for back-charging vendors for their mistakes.

Finally, I would advise that each project team's material specialists become familiar with the "idiosyncrasies" (a polite word in this context) of each country's customs practices. Further, I recommend that the team find and retain a trustworthy local individual who is expert in the local customs practices and who may have contacts in the country's customs organization. It will be worth the time and cost. Often the company that transports the material and equipment from the point of entry to the construction site or point of assembly can provide this service.

I am sure that in reading this, you see the dollar signs required to implement these practices. Believe me that from personal experience, I can say without reservation that these costs should be included in your estimates, or you will spend it many times over, as these companies had been doing.

Accounting

The accounting discipline plays a more important part in the international arena, particularly for companies that do not normally do business abroad. Domestic and foreign tax laws must be understood, or there will be multiple surprises. Because projects are executed over a period of time, that is, many accounting periods, it is important to optimize continually changing currency exchange rates during the processes of procurement, payables, collections, payroll, and internal accounting. Hedging against currency exchange fluctuations in often necessary.

I am not suggesting that project managers become international accountants, but they should make an effort to understand the basics and know what questions to ask and to have a project accountant who has these skills. Early on, I was fortunate to have my company send me to an intensive two-week international management course taught by business school professors. We discussed optimization of currency exchanges, hedging these exchange risks when appropriate, and minimizing the impact of local taxes.

Project managers and their managers should ensure that the company has (or they retain) individuals very familiar with the tax laws in the country where work is done and items are imported. I suggest a reputable local tax consultant who can advise on topics beyond the tax laws. Often localities or government entities will seek to make the rules as they go, and owners will certainly seek to use their influence to optimize their own tax obligations at the project's expense.

Payment terms and designation of the currency in which payments are made requires careful thought. Payments in a local but deflated currency can be costly. My rule of thumb here is to only accept local currency payments in amounts that match the amounts that you will spend in that currency. Even then, try to set the timing in the terms to maintain a neutral local cash flow.

I do recommend to project managers and their managers that they ensure that the accounting done on international projects is performed by people who are fully competent and who are willing to optimize and plan carefully, considering the topics that I have mentioned here and in the upcoming chapter on managers of project managers.

Prime Contract Administration

As I wrote earlier while managing one project in a developing country I attended a contract-signing ceremony that was televised to the entire population. The minister of energy took the stage and announced that the most gracious prime contractor (me) had volunteered to build and staff a training facility for the operators of both the facility we were contracted to build and for their peers at similar facilities in the country. We had not actually volunteered to do this.

The point is that in many countries, the buyer expects to negotiate the scope of large contracts during the course of the contract. There is an expectation that the "rich foreigners" will comply. These expectations are often supported by the contract language, which they will insist upon in a negotiation phase, so that the contract can go on forever.

In many cultures, time is not as important as it is in our society. Most cultures do not share our urgencies. On the other hand, don't be late; even the most laid-back customer will take full advantage of any completion penalties that are provided for.

I should point out that my comments on any of the contract terms I mention here are applicable to all contracts. At the risk of repeating information from chapters 4 and 6, I stress them in this section because, in my experience, international owners supported by local business practices and law are most prone to take full advantage of contract terms that are not explicitly defined.

I have learned that in the international arena, it is particularly important to ensure that the contract terms clearly define the conditions for contract completion milestones. You must avoid terms that are subjective and place the decision as to whether a milestone has been achieved in the hands of the owner. The rich foreigner will be held on the project, sometimes operating and maintaining the project while the owner delays decisions and continually finds new issues, which they will use to either delay acceptance of milestone achievement or to open negotiations, seeking further concessions. As I discussed in chapter 6, these new issues should normally be evaluated as warranty issues and not the basis for contract completion delays.

Other contract terms deserving close attention in this arena are the warranty definition, the disposition of any completion punch list, the payment terms, and the role and authority of any third party supporting the owner. Warranty durations must have a fixed time period and must limit the extent of the remedies to replacement of the defective material and not the labor or indirect/consequential damages, such as temporary unavailability of the project. The designation of any defect must have mutual agreement and not be given to either party. The warranty should avoid any so-called "evergreen" terms, wherein a defect must be corrected many times over.

The use of a punch list is part of the standard project completion process. The contract terms must define that the defects included should be by mutual agreement and be defined to be completed as part of a final inspection process, with a clearly defined closure point, after which any defects will be made part of the warranty process. The completion of the items should be by mutual agreement and definitely not be exclusively in the hands of the owner, who must cooperate by providing reasonable access to the project for completion of the work.

The terms of payment must be defined in such a way as to be totally unambiguous and leave no subjectivity to the owner. These terms should provide for interest on late payments and give the owner no excuses based on the performance of any third party, such as the party's source of financing.

Should the owner retain a third party, such as an engineer, the authority and responsibility of that third party must be clearly defined. I believe that the owner must clearly be responsible for any action or decision taken by the third party. I have had international owners attempt to wash their hands of actions taken by their third-party engineers, seeking to shift the dispute to the two foreign companies.

Chapter 6 deals with cases where all contract-related discussions and negotiations are conducted in the local language. Typically, the buyer can understand you and your internal discussions, but you must communicate through an interpreter. There is lots of room for misunderstandings, which I guarantee will arise later, resulting in disputes that require negotiated settlements.

Local Business Practices and Project Implementation Practices

Soon after beginning a project in a developing county, I was very proud to complete a negotiation on a project issue with the chairman of the national utility that we were dealing with. I was very happy and very naïve. When I followed up some time later, I found that a committee nominated to review all contract changes for the responsible government minister was not satisfied and wanted more concessions. Unfortunately, there was no one that I could negotiate with. The committee had spoken. I complied, only to have the minister himself ask for even more concessions. I learned to understand the approval processes and identify the final authority for any concessions that I was willing to make.

I learned that there was no equity built up in a concession made in a dispute. Unfortunately, I learned that in some cultures, it was best to let the disputes build up, with the goal being a balance in or equal tradeoff in concessions made in what was to be the final negotiation. This applied in both contract negotiations and in the settlement of disputes during the execution phase. These are important lessons about local practices.

Being somewhat defensive, I can say that many years went by without similar errors. But there was one more. Just prior to retiring, I made a deal with a vice president of a reputable foreign company that was large enough to be traded on the New York Stock Exchange. We took the arrangement to our top executives, who blessed the deal in a joint meeting. We even toasted our success with a libation of their choice. When I later visited the country's capital to sign a contract amendment, my "friend," the vice president, would not meet me or even show his face. He sent word that a renegotiation was in order and that it should be handled by our subordinates. The message was clear: understand the practices used locally, don't assume that others hold the ethical business practices that you hold. When possible, use our system. While most foreign executives, as in my stories, will avoid doing so, insist that you write it down when an agreement is made.

I will leave it to others to write about the cultural dos and don'ts, which vary considerably from country to country. There is, however, an important caution about business language, which also varies from culture to culture. Learn what yes really means. Learn what slang, such as "no problem," means locally. Learn what silence really means. Learn about the effect of communicating in either your language or the local language. Learn the proper time of day for business meetings. These lessons, and many more, are all valuable.

Subcontracting

This subject is discussed in chapter 5, devoted to subcontract administration, and in chapter 9, on structuring international projects. To effectively subcontract work scope on international projects, there are a few other considerations that I would like to mention.

Begin by understanding the work practices and methods, as well as the business practices, of potential contractors. Of equal importance is to listen to and understand the preferences of the owner and to understand the relationships between the potential contractors and government or other authorities. Strong relationships between these parties can be good, bad, or both, but you should understand them in any case. For example, close relationships between your contractor and the owner can be effective in resolving disputes, but they can lead to various forms of collusion between the two at your expense. The key is to understand the history of the relationship between the parties. I suggest that you seek and consider the advice of a local agent if your company has one available in the locality.

Determine the owner's or the government's interest in local contracting. Their interest might be to promote local employment, which may be without skills, or to avoid any automation or productivity promoting equipment. This approach could definitely impact your schedule. For example, I have seen workers carrying dirt out of an excavation and bringing concrete for foundations back into the excavation, and pushing spokes of a large wheel in circles to use augers to drive piles. I have seen these and other examples and suffered the schedule impact.

On one project, we were unable to find a suitable general contractor, so we decided to do it ourselves. We used local labor and several dozen expatriates who were to directly train and supervise the locals. Unfortunately, the locals were totally controlled by a tribal leader, with whom we negotiated almost everything, including his share. Take steps to understand the local political environment.

As with domestic work, look at other ongoing or planned work in the area. Internationally, I believe that your labor will readily move from project to project for a few baht, rupees, pesos, or whatever the currency.

Understand the local customs with regard to transportation and feeding and housing workers and their supervisors. Understand how religious customs will affect labor availability. For example, in predominately Muslim countries, progress will definitely slow during Ramadan, the ninth month of the Muslim year. Extended celebrations around the Chinese New Year or a Latin Carnival will have similar effects.

In the international market, you will more often be required to provide skills training. Where you have provided this training, recognize that the trained labor will be very much more valuable and have much more potential to be drawn away to other projects.

While I have not presented a complete checklist of what you should learn about your potential subcontractors and their business and political environment, it should spark your interest in a thorough investigation.

Procurement of Material and Equipment

Certainly, I would not have had to carry suitcases of parts through customs if the supplies or equipment had been procured within the country of interest. Naturally, the most important considerations in selecting vendors are quality and cost and possibly schedule, that is the manufacturing and shipping time.

In the international environment, one should consider procurement locally whenever these three considerations can be satisfied. This will save time, customs delays, and shipping costs, but the customer's interests must be determined in advance. Many international contracts give the owners the right to approve the source of material and equipment. Some customers from developing countries will demand supplies from a developed country, based on a belief that the material or equipment will be of higher quality. Others will embrace the interest of supporting the local economy and local relationships they may have. Considering all of this, my advice is to maintain an ability to procure locally, being mindful of the risks in quality and delivery to meet your schedules.

Be careful of your contract language in this regard. Under one poorly written contract, an executive of a foreign company had the right to approve the selection of all vendors chosen by the project team. He felt that these terms gave him the right to visit every vendor being considered seriously for supply of major equipment on the project. What he really wanted (and what he got) was an all-expense-paid and escorted tour of most of our country and several other countries.

Should you decide to procure locally, I urge that you consider all of the points that I made above in the section on subcontracting in the political and business environment of your customer.

Project Structure

In chapter 9, which is on managers of projects, I will devote considerable time to the structure of large projects. Recognizing that I am a little out of order, I will highlight a few comments on the structure of international projects here. Remember, I said that I would be a little repetitive, so I advise that you read the sections in chapter 9 on organizations and structuring projects in conjunction with this section.

My primary interest in setting the structure for a large international project is to share scope with or subcontract to local companies. Many of the potential pitfalls I discussed in the sections on subcontracting and procurements apply to the selection of partners. Factors like the value of knowing local practices, access to good labor, understanding of local codes and laws, and relationships with the owner and regulatory agencies can be quickly offset by inappropriate relationships or business practices or by poor quality standards or poor schedule performance. Nonetheless, I advise that whenever possible, you deal with local firms.

Often there will be potential partners from third countries who have extensive experience in the country of interest. If you're due diligence verifies sound performance and acceptance by your owners, you should consider this option as preferable to any home country firm without strong local experience. Learning curves are too steep, and it is too time consuming for home country firms to construct local relationships.

Should you select a local or third-country international firm, it is particularly important that you take the time to document the terms and details of the scope split. In the event of their poor performance or default, under a foreign law you will have to rely heavily on this very careful documentation.

Communications

I recognize that technology has dramatically improved our ability to communicate with our staffs in developing countries. On the other hand, I caution you that some of your employees could develop attitudes that make direct communication with the home office quite difficult. This attitude is usually driven by their quest for independence.

Early on, I can remember trying to call home; I was required to have a woman from the owner's office sit with me and monitor the call as I screamed into the only phone circuit for miles, no, kilometers. Conditions certainly have changed.

Only fifteen years before I retired, I assumed responsibility for a construction project in a developing country. The project had a value of several hundred million dollars. There was no direct phone, fax, or electronic communications at our international location. Phone calls could only be made in a municipality almost an hour away. The alternative was an overnight mail service, which took two to three "overnights" to reach the home office. In another case much later, my construction staff had to ride a train a few hours to the nearest town where there was a phone and fax.

Naturally, we corrected these situations with the best technology available at the time, but the local permits, special payments, and the expediting of the services was very time consuming.

The point is that even with the Internet and today's cell phone technology, you should know what the communications options are plan for the cost and set up the best possible communications early. Remember that with today's technology, eavesdropping is a real risk, particularly in countries lacking the controls that we rely on here at home. The rich foreigners are often "fair game."

The Value of Being There

At one company, I assumed responsibility for a number of active international projects, a number of which were in a country where we were required to sponsor a technology transfer to local equipment suppliers, who in turn supplied our projects. Quality and schedule were serious risks with the local companies. I found that the project managers and their supervisors had not visited the local project sites or our local vendors for several months. I promptly visited the construction sites, finding unhappy customers, frustrated employees, and projects in disarray.

I stressed this to project managers in chapter 2 and now make it a very strong point for managers of international projects: being there is a must. The customers expect it. They want to know that the home office is paying attention and there is someone to bring concerns to before situations get out of control. This is particularly important on international projects, where there can be a natural distrust and where there might be reluctance on the part of the project team to travel to the construction site or the international customer. That travel, which your friends and relatives think is so exciting, can quickly become drudgery, stressful, and sometimes dangerous, but it must be done.

From a selfish point of view, the manager of the project's organization absolutely must be present. I have said multiple times that there is a normal tendency on the part of project teams to hide various types of problems. Many unfortunately would not support transparency and would avoid facing the issues and pressures on a failing project. They will delay the exposure for several reasons. It might be the annual bonus. It might be an expected promotion or just fear of the pressure. I believe that it is worth repeating that the site is a gold mine of information. Some information can be gained from just body language, some is observed walking around, some comes from the customer, and some comes from employees who open up for whatever reason (fear, resentment of leaders, being a brown nose). If there are problems, you will sense them. On the other hand, people appreciate your interest in their work and themselves. Bring things to the staff that might be difficult to obtain locally. Spend some relaxed time with them, and listen carefully to their concerns.

Always be sure to visit your customer, both formally and informally. As with your staff, a modest gift that is not normally available to them can bring dividends.

Third-party engineers and financing institution staffs should also receive your attention. A visit where you listen and update them on progress and issues will ease their anxieties. Ignoring them will ensure their bad will and make your life more difficult.

CHAPTER 8
EXTENDED SCOPE PROJECTS

In chapter 1, I briefly outlined some of the more common types of projects, which can be categorized in various ways, usually applying more than one category to a particular project. I outlined several factors that affect the complexity of a project, some of which are given special attention in this book. In that chapter, I defined an extended scope project as one involving contributions from multiple disciplines, generally in sequence. These contributions are typically integrated, one supporting another, necessitating a limited amount of overlap. The necessary integration of the engineering and procurement activity is a good example.

Examples of the various disciplines are conceptual engineering, design, procurement, detailed engineering, fabrication, transportation, construction, testing, training, and commissioning. Complexity is added when the disciplines are from different companies, requiring contracts or formal agreements to define the scope and relationships.

The material that I discuss in this book applies to a wide range of projects, including extended scope projects. Before you manage such a project, I recommend that you gain experience managing projects using a single or a few disciplines, beginning with a project where all disciplines come from within the same company.

Extended scope projects take a giant step in complexity when, to accelerate the schedule, the discipline contributions overlap each other, often with multiple overlaps for any one discipline. Then the fun starts. These are usually referred to as "fast track" projects.

Skills and processes for integrated sequencing and scheduling, for progress measurement, for contract and subcontract administration, and for communication are of particular value. As the leader of an extended scope fast track project, you will have serious risks. For example, when one party or discipline delays or works out of sequence, impacting another discipline, the impacted party will typically hold you accountable, as you are the party with whom they have a contractual relationship. Typically these parties do not have contractual relationships between themselves. You, the prime contract manager, will pay for the mistakes or delays that impact any of the contributing disciplines.

Even with the best scheduling skills, you will be seriously challenged when trying to have the various parties agree to commit and then work to the sequences and timing required by the party they are supporting. The parties will have to commit to details in work sequence and work completion that are not required in typical single-discipline projects. For this commitment, the parties will seek to minimize their risk with lenient contract terms.

Under fast track conditions, when one party misses commitments, it is usually difficult to hold them accountable because they will seek to blame the party that they relied upon for input. With so many detailed transactions, sorting it all out requires outstanding planning skills, performance tracking processes, and finally contract administration.

Communications and strong relationships are critical in order to allow for the inevitable changes in the program sequences and priorities, thereby avoiding disputes, claims, and counterclaims. Inappropriate handling of the parties could result in an informal alliance against you. Be careful.

To deal with this type of contract, the hard work is done up front. Develop with each discipline very detailed sequencing of the work, which will support the timing and work sequence of the follow-on party. Where iterative processes are necessary, define and get agreement to the process from the parties involved. Insist that the parties support detailed progress tracking systems. Where you feel comfortable with the attitudes of any parties, you should allow direct communication between them to avoid delays in communication through your team.

Keep in mind that forcing individual parties to commit to your sequences and timing will lead to failure. Take the time to work with the affected parties to find accommodations to each other. Remember that most parties will build extra time or float into their schedules. Your job is to find the time or, if necessary, to make accommodations where they need it. Again remember that because of the extent of integration between the parties, the parties have a stronger position from which to avoid contractual actions against them. They will blame others, who are directly or contractually under your responsibility.

One or more of the integrated disciplines or parties will be from your company, so you must first ensure that their performance is fully responsive to the needs of the others. My experience, unfortunately, is to the contrary. Internal components serving both internal and external customers will give priority to the external customers, where there is usually a contract to be satisfied. Internally, there is usually just a little "heat" when commitments are not met.

Be sure that all parties are kept aware of the status of the overall project, including all of the critical issues. Hiding this or, worse, asking a party to meet dates that are earlier than realistically needed, will lead to distrust and a lack of the necessary team cooperation.

Turnkey projects, fast track or not, are extended scope projects that include all of the disciplines necessary so that the customer can take control or occupancy and immediately have beneficial use. This type of project is simply defined by the full extent of the scope.

Turnkey projects do not have to be fast track, and preferably they are not. Turnkey projects can have any single or combination of the standard types of payment terms. Industrial projects are often referred to as Lump Sum Turnkey (LSTK) projects.

The management of turnkey projects is not much more complex than an extended scope project with multiple disciplines. The difference is the integration of the testing and commissioning phase, typically along with the training of the owner's staff. This requires that your company retain or have access to the additional skills necessary. In my opinion the greatest risks are with the owners who will seek to hold you for extended periods of operation by abusing the acceptance criteria.

In a way, I relate turnkey projects to a situation many years ago. After serving as project manager for construction of a full power prototype of a submarine propulsion system, I was invited to go along on a sea trial. To me, this was the ultimate test of the quality of my team's contributions to the design, construction, and training of the crew. I enjoyed the experience and am here to tell about it. In turnkey projects, the contractor must stay and measure the quality of the work through the testing and initial operation of the project. I have had many turnkey projects where acceptance by the owner required not only successful performance testing but also an extended period of successful and uninterrupted operation. There is no other party who is directly responsible to the owner for the success of the project.

CHAPTER 9.

FOR THE MANAGER OF PROJECTS

This chapter focuses on managers of project organizations that are directly managing project managers under their direct supervision, a position that is, in my opinion, much less enjoyable than being the project manager itself. I will give my experience and conclusions regarding the organizational approach, considering concepts like the project island, a way of arranging the project teams physically, the matrix organizations, the use of project bonuses, staffing and structuring projects, and so forth.

I will dwell on the importance of the information flow to the manager of projects and the importance of common procedures and methods by all project units. These two critical practices will be the key drivers in deciding on the manager's organizational approach.

I will then highlight several of the previously discussed process subjects, which are of particular interest to the individual responsible for project success by others. I will try to stress the way the managers should require the processes to be implemented.

As you, the manager of projects, approach this chapter, remember that while yours is a bigger glass, it is even more important that you consider it to be half empty.

Defining Your Organization

You, as the leader of the project organization, do not have time to deal with a number of different project managers and teams, each of whom is at a different point on the learning curve, has different processes, has different thresholds for taking action, and most importantly has a different plan and format for reporting on the state of the project, particularly the financial state. Remember, most project teams will avoid disclosing problems and will therefore use their skills to invent reports that exclude points that might be troublesome to them.

When I took on the manager position in two different large organizations, I found lots of individuals managing projects their way, hiring and training teams to do it their way, right or wrong. In one case, I was confronted with a consolidation of project execution organizations from different parts of the company, each of whom had a different set of processes (usually from undocumented procedures). In each case, there was chaos and literally no flow of easily digestible information. I needed to be able to focus on key variances to project plans, assuming those plans existed, and be able to have consistent process expectations and receive the information in a consistent format.

To accomplish this, I strongly recommend a matrix organization, using functional subgroups that are responsible to hire and train staffs and to prepare standard procedures to be used by the staffs. These functional groups will assign personnel to individual project teams, monitor the performance of the individuals, and ensure compliance of the project teams to the standard procedures. The functional leaders should prepare (or have significant input into) the performance evaluations of the assigned individuals.

The functional groups can be defined in many ways. Typically, I would use construction, commissioning or startup, contract administration, general administration, engineering, planning and scheduling, cost forecasting, and project accounting, but the structure will depend on the type of project and size of the organization. The only guidance that I would give would be to assign the project accountants, who are totally separate from the cost forecasters (cost engineers), to the corporate accounting function, the controller.

In smaller organizations, the functional groups can be combined for cost efficiency. An additional way to address the cost restraints is to arrange for different project teams to share the services of a single functional staff member.

Using this approach, a matrix of functional support units with the project teams will ensure that the leader of the organization does not waste time sorting out whether there is a variance to plans, which saves the leader much of the anxiety associated with wondering whether all of the right things are being done.

The matrix approach with functional groups has the additional advantage of providing independent oversight, both by the trained staff assigned to the project and the functional leaders. In addition, the functional leader can provide for a balance in the strength of the various project teams by the thoughtful assignment of the staff.

It may sound like, by endorsing a matrix approach, I am in some way dividing the responsibility for project performance and not holding the project manager fully responsible for the ultimate outcome. No, this is not the case at all. The team members are assigned to the project manager for all project-related direction. Project managers should have the responsibility to release nonperformers, and when a standard procedure does not apply, they have the duty to come to the manager of projects for a change.

I have found organization structures that purposefully separated project responsibilities among leaders within the project. Specifically, project implementation, that is, the supply of scope to meet schedule, was separated from all project commercial responsibilities. My observation was that this was purposefully done to avoid giving responsibility for the outcome of the project to any one individual. This objective was achieved, as projects got in trouble in one area or the other (or both of these areas). Leadership accountability was lost.

The project manager must, however, understand that some detailed decisions must be left with functional leaders. For example, in the engineering and design process, the internal manager of the engineering unit must have the ultimate responsibility. This is to ensure that codes and design standards are met and the company's interests are protected. Project managers might challenge a design, based on cost or schedule considerations, if they see fit and identify the out-of-budget cost as a cost variance assignable to engineering. However, the final decision on designs should be with the functional manager.

The organization structure must be complemented with an understanding by all that the project manager has the overall responsibility on the project.

The next concept that I would strongly endorse is that of a project island. This is the physical consolidation of the various members of a team, large or very small, into one area. This approach is compatible with the more conventional team structure or with the matrix approach that I have described. While not absolutely necessary for success when using the matrix approach, the project island approach will enhance team unity, communication, and ownership of the outcome.

By grouping team members in an area where there is a community or conference atmosphere, communication is dramatically enhanced. Overheard telephone calls or conversations heard over the partitions can lead to unexpected solutions. Impromptu meetings can occur quickly for urgent topics. There is no delay for mailing hard copy, and a team member who is too lazy to find others to communicate with should no longer be a problem. Finally, posted communication, such as progress photos, help develop team unity and dedication. No one can hide.

Regular project team meetings should be mandatory and help with communication, but they do not match the project island approach in effectiveness by a wide margin.

I have tried all manner of organization structures for projects and conclude that the matrix with a project island is clearly the most effective, no matter what size the team is. As an auditor at a company delivering engineered software on a project basis, I found every discipline, even the project managers, located separately. I had never seen such poor communication. While there, I tried to help by carrying messages and deliver news whenever possible.

Developing Consistent and Accurate Information Flow

Do you remember my comments on the value of a strong information system that I learned from Admiral Rickover? His system caused me to stop and think about what were the most important things to spend time on. This was done through preparation for regular written and oral reports. Preparation was the key word.

I implemented this through regular structured project review meetings for project managers and by requiring that other managers give me what I called critical items reports.

With this background and my own experience, I learned that the leader of any project organization must hold reviews of each and every project using a standard agenda and standard documentation. These reviews should be held at least monthly. The functional leaders and key members of the project team should attend these meetings.

The key ingredient is a very structured and detailed report on all aspects of the project, financial and otherwise. As I said earlier, as the manager of projects, I wanted to know that the project manager had looked at all elements of the project activities every month. I cannot tell you how often I found that a problem developed and grew because of a "lack of a look." In the heat of battle, it is easy to ignore the key issues for the team's attention, to not look at the age of inquiries from contractors, to not look at the progress in resolving claims on vendors, and on and on.

In my experience, no single necessary practice in project management has been opposed more than the structured periodic review meetings and critical items reports. Managers do not want to spend the time. Project managers really do not want the exposure. In meetings with teams and groups of individuals to talk about our business in general, including whatever they wanted to talk (or complain) about, the predominant complaint was usually the need to prepare for these monthly reports.

I can tell you that my commitment to the review process can be measured by the fact that I would spend up to three or four days a month conducting these reviews. I can also say with pride that a number of project-based organizations implemented this process after observing the results that we had.

Often it was suggested that I use reports submitted by the project teams in lieu of meeting with project managers to review the reports. Don't be fooled, I regularly learned as much from the body language, conflicting comments, or questioning glances as I did from the reports. Based on my observations and questions, I would learn who was really running the project, who knew what was going on, who deserved recognition, and who was wasting my time. I would learn whether the functional leaders were contributing with their oversight and with their training.

In structuring the reports to be presented at these review meetings, the nature of your business is very important, but there are many common themes. I wanted to ensure a look at all areas, but more importantly, I wanted project managers to comment on the status/progress in many areas and tell me where their time should be spent. As I said earlier, "markups" or "cut and paste" from a prior review and report was never allowed.

I wanted to know about topics like critical issues, team staffing issues, and progress—in the words of the key player in each of the functional areas (numbers are good but I wanted it in the words of the key people). I wanted a look at claims and counterclaims, both up (owners) and down (subcontractors) in the contract hierarchy. I asked for commentary and detail on project risks and opportunities, both financial and otherwise. I wanted to know that they were looking at the various communications that can backlog. I wanted to see trends in the causes of cost variances or nonconformance.

To me, transparency at all levels and from all players is absolutely critical to any project's success. Not only should the leader of the project's organization accept nothing else from the team and its support cast, but also the leader must implement systems, procedures, and oversight at various levels to ensure this transparency.

Most did not see the value to themselves, and the project, of stopping and thinking about the important issues, the important risks, what the numbers really meant, and to touch for a moment or two on all key topics and measures within the project. They did not see the value in thinking enough to be able to write and be questioned about the critical topic. Writing down your thoughts and the results of your look at all areas is a key part of the process.

I had learned the value of these processes after some serious complaining myself as a young manager. I learned that they were necessary, even if the "boss" did not demand it. I came to know the value of thoughtful introspection, even if it meant skipping the in-flight movie or sleeping on a flight to a construction site, vendor, or customer.

In the project review meetings, I was able to learn who had really done their homework and who was open and transparent in their reports. Reviews with these individuals were generally quick to the point and a constructive experience for us all. On the other hand, in cases where I had developed a lack of confidence in someone's completeness and transparency, I would probe more, and you would never know what would come up.

Certainly I did not have time to get into all details in all the project reports, so I learned to look at faces, numbers, and words and the answers to a few questions to know where to look further.

I learned the value of asking a few questions, and if I was concerned about the direct answer (or even the body language), I probed further. Some individuals got few questions from me, and others felt that there was an interrogation going on. In addition to forcing transparency so that the real issues would be addressed, I used this time to evaluate individuals and to teach. With many individuals, most of whom I could not interact with regularly, this was my chance to get to know them. Teaching may have been the most productive part of the meeting. Paradoxically I found myself devoting time to teaching the most capable, those with most potential. They were the future of the organization.

For those not involved in monthly reporting on a complete project, I would require a periodic letter telling me what they thought was the most critical element within their scope of responsibility. These individuals—site managers, functional managers, and the like—were to add what action they should take when identifying a critical issue. The goal was to get them to spend their time where it was most needed, but it often exposed surprises hidden by others.

Finally on the subject of information flow, I will tell you that I set my priorities by the input I received, and I was generally much more capable of quickly responding to inquiries from my superiors, often from the top of my head.

Construction and Vendor Site Visits

In addition to the importance of spending time on the reviews I just mentioned, I believe strongly that I could not effectively manage the organization from the hallowed halls of the home office. I have seen many try and fail, some miserably. I concluded that good morale was enhanced by these visits, which would always produce surprises, making the trip worthwhile.

When you assign people to work off-site, be it at a construction site, a factory, an engineering office, or the like, they want to know that someone in the home office is thinking of them and that their unique problems are being addressed. Their concerns are generally valid. Frankly, some introspection into myself revealed a stronger personal link to the folks making the sacrifice of being away. I have found that a short visit, including an open group meeting, can be very helpful. Listen to their problems and tell them what is going on in the company and the home office. Make time to invite the team to lunch or dinner or for a libation after work. This will help in a very different way.

Naturally, a site or area tour led by your leader(s) will bring you a better understanding of the true progress and circumstances at the location. Sometimes, you will find differences from your expectations that are based on the reviews at home. In addition, this would give me an abundance of good questions for the next monthly review. From the tour, you will also get a good evaluation of the folks you are relying on.

At one point after consolidating projects in my organization, I visited one of the new project sites. The project was in progress and in financial difficulty. Upon arrival, I asked to take a walking tour of the works. The project manager, however, decided that he had better things to do than to walk with me. Troubled, I found a later opportunity that he could not refuse. I found that he really did not know the work, the real issues, and the program plans. He never made another walk of the project, as he was promptly relieved. I had found one good reason for the project's troubles.

I have also had many cases where people at the locations that I visited found a way to tell me what was really going on. No matter what the source or their motive, I was always grateful for the opportunity to evaluate and research what I have been told. There was always plenty of good information.

When visiting locations, leave your tie at home. Dress as you would expect your leaders to dress and be prepared to walk, crawl, or climb wherever they take you. I have spent hours in subzero conditions or climbing to the highest structure just to see what needed to be seen or to pass the tests given to me by some.

Finally, don't forget to visit the customer with your most senior local leader, if there is a customer representative at the location. Visit them no matter what their position in the customer's hierarchy. As the customer's leader, they will appreciate the recognition, and you will be surprised at what you will learn. My only caution would be to not take issues fully out of the hands of your team. Keep them visible in any resolutions of customer issues. Your staff has to stay, and you do not want to have all of the future customer's issues brought to you.

Structuring Individual Projects Involving Multiple Entities

One of my mentors once told me that there is no such thing as a partnership, because "someone always gets screwed." I think this was a little overstated, but it taught me to be very cautious in selecting companies to work with, in the project structures I sponsored, and in my documentation of the proceedings within a multi-company project structure. Even then, I made many mistakes.

On large and complicated projects with potentially partnered functions, such as construction, engineering, and procurement, or subcontracted arrangements for these functions, there will always be the question of how to structure, that is legally combine, the participating entities. The incorrect answer to these questions has ruined many a project and, frankly, some companies.

Certainly, I will not attempt to recommend a specific manner to divide work or set up arrangements for subcontracts or partnering agreements. No one size fits all. This can be very complicated, considering questions like subcontract versus partnering, structure of the partnership (e.g., split scope and price or shared scope in a so-called joint venture), or the placement of the entities in the hierarchy of the project execution organization. I will, however, provide some guidance for the project team in making these decisions.

Frankly, I have never liked arrangements wherein each party has its own scope and its own price without some terms that interrelate the risks and provide incentives for each party to assist the other and avoid alliances with the owner at the other party's expense. I have repeatedly seen such arrangements fail. I prefer arrangements where the scope split and risk is equally divided and where both parties are jointly responsible to the owner for meeting the terms of the prime contract.

There are many reasons for considering some form of alliance or subcontract arrangement. Often, customers will ask for the involvement of a firm in the project, because they like the firm's work or because of a special relationship or payback of some form. Be cautious; customers have a way of forgetting their requests when problems arise. In international locations or those controlled by certain companies or labor organizations, it can be valuable to share scope in some way with the local entities.

At times, it is reasonable to reduce the price in bidding a project by avoiding a major procurement, with its associated margins at two levels (yours and the vendor). Such a step would avoid the need for the prime company to mark up the procurement in order to meet internal risk management or margin guidelines. This can be done by bringing the vendor onto the team to share in the potential upside in the financial outcome. Typically, the vendor will be more cooperative in such an arrangement.

Most often, the initiative to share participation with others is driven by the prime contractor itself. Special skills may be needed, or there may be financially driven motives. The prime may not have sufficient or specialized skills, may want to share the risks, or may need the backing of a larger company to meet bonding or letter of credit requirements.

No matter what the reason to share the scope of supply in a project, there are a few basic guidelines that I have developed for myself. First, absolutely, you should minimize the number of process interfaces. For example, do not separate the entity specifying any engineered components from the entity buying the equipment. Delays are guaranteed as the information is passed through several iterations of engineering approvals and the use of the vendor's detail in system designs.

Certainly do not separate the engineering and design in different locations or even divide the engineering into different companies or locations. Giving the "lower end" portion of the engineering of an integrated project to a less expensive engineering company will cost more in the end. For example, I would not separate the design of pipe hanger details from the supply of these engineered devices.

As another example, if given the choice I would not separate the construction responsibility from the commissioning of the equipment or systems.

In the construction area, I would give the construction contractor the responsibility for the engineering/design and procurement of systems and facilities that are not critical to the function of any basic deliverable. This would eliminate interfaces that could put you between two participants when claims and disputes arise.

As a further step in controlling interfaces, I advise avoiding the management of multiple contractors as a prime, unless the prime is an experienced general contractor. Look at avoiding conflicts in the use of space by contractors. If multiple contractors are necessary in the same space, look at pre-contract agreements on the use of alternate work times (different shifts)

Clear lines of authority and decision making are another must. When forming a partnership, say a joint venture, be absolutely clear in the agreement about who has the individual responsibility to make decisions for the partnership. The norm, evolving from basic distrust, is to give the authority to some form of joint committee or vote, with each party having equal weight. If there is not enough trust to allow one company to take control, then there should not be a partnership between them.

On the other hand, it is good to have a management committee follow the progress and working relationships within the organization and make decisions when necessary to keep the peace and maintain constructive relationships. This latter approach is also a way to keep the management close to the project.

In dividing the scope between the parties, do so on the basis of expertise. If the parties insist on dividing it based on percentages of the scope, I can assure you that the risk of problems will go up substantially. Project leadership does not demand that one entity have the largest share, as long as the terms of risk sharing and profit and loss are written equitably. If dividing the scope on the basis of expertise results in a party having a very small share, consider contracting to that party.

Scope definition is another discipline that requires attention. I have seen many failures when partners of prime contractors attempted to split the scope on a conceptual basis. That is like inviting the lawyers to lunch. When the agreements are finalized at the outset of the project, it is imperative that the scope documents have great detail. Use lists of equipment, components, and documents marked-up drawings; descriptions of the processes; and the like. Lists and definitions made by the people most familiar with the scope, not contract administrators or salespeople, are necessary.

I would avoid partnering with a much larger and financially stronger company. When problems arise, the "bully" often comes to play, and the situation can easily get worse for you. I would strongly advise that the level of risks taken be normalized against the financial strengths of the participating partners.

Some partnerships or joint ventures rely on an independent neutral party to resolve routine disputes. The only way I favor this is to give the neutral party the responsibility to give a position on any dispute and to require that this position be the tie-breaking vote or a compromise that must be accepted. In this arrangement, it is reasonable to set a very substantial dollar value, over which the dispute goes back to the management. Neutral parties as advisors without authority just do not work.

I am also against dispute resolution language which gives disputes to a higher level of each party's management for prompt resolution. These highly paid people typically are not close enough, do not have the time, or just want to wait and see the overall situation at the project completion before committing to a decision.

The documentation that defines the responsibilities and relationships between the parties is the most important consideration in developing the partnership. Recently I audited a project where there were at lease six different documents defining the relationship between the two partners and the owners. This included a summary contract and individual contracts between the owner and the two prime parties. There were consortium agreements and scope agreements, all without a clear statement of the order of precedence. It was silly, risky to all, and probably the product of a contract or sales group who did not have to execute the project. I recommend letting the project implementation people develop the working documents that they will have to use and provide for a legal review as a supplement.

I have seen the best results with a single customer contract, with one party combined with a single detailed agreement between the parties in the partnership.

Measuring Project Costs Individually

Implicit in what I stressed in chapter 3 on the subject of cost plans and measurements is the requirement to measure the financial performance of each project individually. At three separate companies that I either joined or assumed responsibility as the manager of projects, I was very surprised to find one overall measure of profit and loss for the entire organization.

Unless you can measure each project's profitability individually and have one responsible individual on each project, there will be no accountability. Further, when there is a single companywide measure, the data necessary to quantify nonconforming or non-budgeted cost is not available, the ability to distinguish between good and poor performance is very difficult, and there is a clear opportunity to misrepresent the company's profitability.

As mentioned earlier, I found organization structures that purposefully separated a project's overall performance responsibility from its commercial responsibility in a so-called two-headed leadership. The project manager was given overall (noncommercial) responsibility, and a commercial manager was in charge of commercial aspects, including cost management. In another organization, a member of the company's financial staff did the cost forecasts instead of the project team. In both of these cases, there was an attempt at cost measurement on individual projects, but because of the structure and responsibility assignments, the cost reports and forecasts were not accurate and could not truly be owned by anyone. The result was that neither party understood the true financial situation or was accountable for project performance as a whole. In my mind, these arrangements were made purposefully so that there could not be a single individual accountable on a project or so that senior management could abuse the process of entries into the company ledger.

In these organizations, some of the project managers were ignorant of cost issues. This encouraged others to make cost issues on individual projects invisible. Without individual measurements, the project leaders were unaccountable and were usually able to earn points with their customers by overspending and some form of giveaway.

As I related earlier in one company, the division manager continually asked, "Where the cost bleeding was" but no one wanted to tell, could tell, or had an incentive to tell him. No one had full individual responsibility. What a mess. In another company, the controller had no good information from people on the various projects and relied in part on people in engineering or procurement, who wanted recognition for their cost-saving ideas or savings in the procurement process. The controller often used these so-called "savings" to improve the company's margins. He did not stay very long.

I have seen other companies rely on audit teams to determine the real financial status of the project and the expected financial outcome. Believe me, any good project manager can lead an auditor to the wrong conclusions. This is particularly true without a good process for identifying cost risks, accounting for out-of-budget or so-called nonconformance costs, and continually updating the project's cost forecast at completion, all of which I have discussed.

In addition to using the project team's knowledge, there must be accountability within the project team for the fiscal status and for the projected cost at completion. This forecasted cost at completion should be the only basis on which the company accounting can make entries into the financial register. Even in the engineering company where projects delivered engineered material, such accountability and cost management on a project-by-project basis was recognized to be necessary.

Staffing the Projects

In general, staffing in a project business is based on the same principles and practices as in any other business, with the exception of a few added elements. There must be thoughtful selection to ensure a match between the key project management traits and the individual, combined with job-specific training and career development programs.

If you are evaluating an individual's potential for project management, I suggest you review the traits I discussed in chapter 2. They should believe that all contributors are not equal, that surprises will happen, and that whatever can go wrong, will go wrong; it is also essential that they are willing to plan for all eventualities. A willingness to plan in a detailed way and focus on detail when measuring progress such that the issues can be easily identified is also important. They should also be willing and able to travel routinely.

In the section on international projects, I commented on staffing. I stressed the importance of comfort and experience in the international area as well as the best balance between company employees and contractor "hired guns" when there is a shortage of international experience in the home office. I will refer you back to chapter 7 and not repeat all of that advice here.

I have suggested in the above section on organization that the responsibility for staffing and training of new hires be done by the functional leaders who will have the long-term responsibility for their development and performance. The career horizon for the hires should be well beyond the duration of any project. I would avoid allowing project managers to do their own hiring; they should not have the time, and they often do not have the proper background for it. I have seen cases where employees hired by a project manager expect to stay with that manager, who may have his or her own individual methods, destroying the principle of everyone doing it the same way and limiting the potential for growth of the individual in the broader organization.

In the case of project managers, I have always had a preference for homegrown people, as long as "home" has the ability to grow them. I have had the opportunity to develop a career path template for project managers. The career path defined training and experience requirements, which were quite specific, with milestones and prerequisites. Such a plan is valuable and should be matched to the company and its services.

Managing a large, say multimillion dollar, project with multiple contributing functions requires the same skills as managing a small profit center. Training and development is therefore a must. I strongly suggest a combined career development program for young employees and menus of required training and position experiences for more senior people. Such a program should be flexible but include a combination of training and self-study to be reviewed by a qualified project manager. More importantly, the program must include assignments to field positions, engineering, procurement, junior project positions, and the like, depending on the specific business. I believe that the field experience is the most important.

I believe that project managers should have training in basic accounting as well as the company's accounting practices. A very deep and strong technical knowledge of the company's products is not necessary and certainly not a prerequisite for the position. Project skills are more important, but a good familiarity with the product is necessary.

I have seen many engineers trained as technicians assume that the project is all about the technology or equipment; they fail at project management because they do not have the project management skills or cannot break away from the technical details. This deep technical knowledge can often become a simple distraction.

The Best Approach to Proper Compensation

The potential impact of the project's success on the company as a whole and the skills required must be considered in setting the compensation of the project leadership. In addition to properly setting the base salary so as to recognize the project's impact on the overall business and the experience and skill required, I recommend a carefully thought-out incentive program for both the project leadership and key members of the project team. I say "carefully thought-out," because I have seen many failed incentive programs. To me the key elements are to provide an incentive to continue on the project team and to provide an incentive to the team for strong performance by rewarding them at the end of a successful project.

I stress the end because I have had poor experience with interim bonuses, say an annual bonus on a longer-term project. Unfortunately, such bonuses motivate the teams to manage the project and the performance data to match the interim goals, irrespective of the longer term situations. A bonus at project completion will serve to keep team members, who might otherwise move elsewhere prior to the end of the project, working on the project.

In structuring the incentive plan, the most important point is to gain a "buy in" from the team so that the program goals and thresholds are seen to be a stretch yet achievable by the team members. Naturally, there should never be a reward for failing to meet the as-sold profit objective of the company or the conditions sold to the customer. Don't get trapped into negotiating a reward for any failure against the basic expectations of the customer or your company. Further, don't allow yourself to become emotional, make or support excuses, and pay a bonus anyway. Doing so can easily have a counter motivating effect throughout the organization. Believe me, I know.

I recommend providing an incentive for all project positions, with a sliding scale for their value to the project. Allow the project team to have some flexibility in adjusting the bonuses paid to team members, recognizing variations in contribution. They know best who the best contributors were.

Finally, there is the value of the incentive offered. The value must be substantial if it is to cause the required effect. Token amounts are a waste of time. Special dinners, letters of recognition, or plaques just will not do. The potential amount must be large enough to have an impact on the employee's quality of life. Remember that circumstances, sometimes out of the control of the team, will eliminate the bonus potential, making them wait for another opportunity. I suggest setting financial outcome as the primary performance element in the bonus system. If properly set, the bonus will be for excess margin or profit made by the company. In this case, the company should share a portion of the excess, thereby allowing for a substantial value of the bonus.

One of your hurdles in developing a project performance incentive system is liable to be your company's existing bonus policy. The bureaucrats will not want a new system for any type of compensation. They will work to force it into the existing system and weaken the incentives. All I can recommend is that you be persistent as leader of the project organization and find a believer in your incentive proposal who is higher up in your organization.

Pay Attention to Pre-Contract Activity

As the manager of the project implementation activity in your company, you must be allowed by the company structure to not only participate in the pre-contract activity but to have a say (even an approval authority) in the process.

In most large projects, there are three arenas of concern in the decision to submit a specific bid: cost estimating, feasibility of the technical scope to be supplied and the commercial risk assessment. In the areas of pricing, that is margins above cost, risk in the technical offering, and risk in the contract terms, both general and legal, your company should have standards against which the proposed contract should be measured. You must be involved in the cost estimate assuring that all hidden scope is included and in all of the variances against the standards for legal and commercial terms. You must ensure that a strong attempt has been made to objectively identify the cost risks and opportunities. You should also be responsible for providing the cost of implementing the project by your team in the pre-bid estimate. I believe that your role should be to support the company in obtaining work, taking contracts that stretch your capability, and ensuring that the cost and variances to company standards for terms and technology are reasonable.

Your success will depend on the culture of your company and the level of any desperation that there might be to win work. If your company is balanced with an effective risk management program, you will probably be successful in making the necessary contributions. Once I was responsible for both winning and implementing project activity, I was quite successful relying mostly on our strategies and our customer relationships.

Unfortunately, some of my experience was with companies with sales-dominated cultures. Yes, there were risk management processes that focused on the variances to company standards, but the system was undermined at various levels. The sales and marketing team would campaign vigorously to cut the properly determined cost estimates. They would make concessions in scope, hiding them in the general or specific contract terms, where there were no company standards for the specific topic. These same people would work very hard to frame the variances to company standards such that the risks were understated (or not identify a variance to standards at all).

At the senior management level, decisions were often made to just get the work, basically ignoring the standards. Frankly, I could accept and support the latter at times, for long-term projects when work was desperately needed. Winning the work would hold the company together and provide an opportunity to find profitable and lower risk work in the future. I say "at times," because I believed that this high-risk approach was taken all too often.

Should you work at a company with such a culture, my advice is to persevere but cautiously. Caution is necessary or you might be eliminated from the process, as I was eliminated at one point.

My bottom line here is to have your company implement a pre-contract process that has careful review and formal acceptance of the cost estimate and the variances to company standards for acceptable risk in the technology offered and the contract terms to be accepted. With this in place, you must allow time to participate fully in the process.

Does the Legal Staff Always Share Your Goals?

My relationships with the legal community have spanned a very wide spectrum of trust and respect. Most of this is to my account, because I was unable to understand why the legal process was not simply a matter of telling the truth and deciding issues on that basis; naïve, I guess.

My major concern and advice relates to the processes for mediation, arbitration, and litigation, particularly when the lawyers are being paid by the hour, with the cost being applied to the project.

I will always remember a case that I thought was strong in our favor. I went to mediation and was able to reach a settlement. Unfortunately, an attorney who thought he could get a better settlement through arbitration shared the opinion of my boss. Guess what? We ultimately lost on every point in arbitration; I still wonder about the attorney's motivation.

No discipline that I have dealt with can expand the work on a particular activity as can the legal profession. As a manager of projects, I would almost desperately look for ways to settle disputes, avoiding the legal processes even at the expense of concessions that I did not consider to be necessary. I did this because of my experience with dispute resolution, arbitration, and litigation processes, which always seemed to create unreasonable expense and delay.

Dispute resolution through the legal procedures involved endless exchange of documents, research, interviews or depositions, development of extensive legal documents, posturing, and a charade called mediation, and hearings or trials in court. It was expensive and frustrating and very distracting from my real job. I advise avoiding it at all cost.

I often concluded that the matters were so technical and complex that a panel, typically lawyers, or a jury would compromise in their decision, giving each party something to feel good about. I feel that this is why many parties lacking a good case lean toward arbitration or litigation. They would rely on and be satisfied with a piece of the pie.

In my work experience and my experience as an expert witness, I have had other distasteful experiences. Time after time, I observed attorneys and other so-called experts present positions that I know they could not have believed themselves. Since attorneys are not typically under oath, we rely on their ethics, yet I observed lies, misleading statements, omissions, and defamations of witnesses and experts, seeming anything to extend their billing hours and to win the case.

As I said earlier, you should avoid turning the settlement decision over to others, even when the legal community promises you success through the legal process. My experience on routine matters was usually good, but I did encounter attorneys who just would not commit to a specific recommendation when I needed it. These individuals would give me alternatives with a comment on each. I recognize that I was being paid to make the decisions, but I wanted clear legal advice that I could balance with the commercial or political situations.

My advice is to balance all of the considerations and make your decision, allowing the attorney to tell you if it is legally correct or not.

Other Process Items of Particular Interest to be Considered

If you are a manager of projects and jumped to this chapter, I encourage you to returning to chapter 3 and read it carefully. No matter what the size or complexity of a project, the processes outlined there are the most valuable material herein. I said this was not a process manual and so have only functionally outlined the processes of planning and management of variances from the plans. You should understand these processes yourself, train your staffs, and enforce their use diligently and without exception.

If you need to find resources, either material or instructors, to ensure your success, do so. There are many resources available on the Internet, many books available, and many consultants and trade associations ready to pitch in. One company I worked for spent millions developing training material based on internal processes being used, training instructors, and requiring participation in the training. Unfortunately, in my opinion, the project team organization and structure and the decision making policies within the project teams were flawed; they were eventually changed.

Once your staff is trained, they will fail in implementation without access to procedures for standard processes as well as the automation and systems necessary. Beyond the hardware, they will require software systems for integrated scheduling and cost budgeting, tracking, and forecasting. These applications must be integrated with each other and must be integrated with your company's cost accounting system. The scheduling system must provide for critical path measurement and provide for weighting, allowing for the measurement of overall progress.

I recommend software for data management, allowing for managing the "list of lists" and the extensive correspondence and documents that will be required.

Remember that the key to project management is being able to devote your attention to the areas needing it most. This can only be done by detailed planning and measurement of the performance against those plans. Having this capability, the next things that can threaten you are those who do not abide by the contracts and subcontracts that your teams will rely on.

Chapters 4 and 5 and the sections of chapter 6 that deal with relationships with the customer are also worth reviewing. Again, I have tried only to hit the highlights, or warned against the low lights from my experience. I suggest you staff your organization for good project administration and have your staffs trained by professionals.

At this point, I have had you review most of the book, so why not continue with chapter 6? Look at my responses to cost issues and the topics on project closeout. The latter is often forgotten until the job just never ends.

CHAPTER 10.

WRAP IT UP

At this point, you have probably figured out why the title of this book is what it is.

Over the years, influenced by those who were successful at what they did and my own experiences, I learned to believe that if it could go wrong, it often would, and that some people I encountered (within or outside my teams) would be operating with less than the most laudable and supportive motives. Some will seek to enhance both their own personal positions within their company and their company's position relative to others, often by doing whatever they can get away with. Sure, there are many things that go very well, particularly if you plan and don't rely on prayer, luck, or hope, and there are many outstanding people who are always seeking to do the right thing. The problem is that you cannot act as if all will miraculously go well; you must realize that the nontrivial number of bad-intentioned and poor-performing people could undermine your project, which is very important to your company and your career.

If you can agree that a small number of assumptions and plans will not turn out as expected or that even a small number of people will not support your goals with the commitment that you expect, you must conclude that you must be prepared for these unexpected situations with your planning, attitude, and follow-up.

If you are not sure about my half-empty glass and my pessimistic approach, consider the economic situation that developed in our country from 2007 through 2009. Most people agree that it was caused by a combination of potential homeowners who did not do their homework (or who wanted something for nothing) and businesspeople that failed to follow accepted practice and who took advantage of others for their personal gain. People cannot always be relied upon to do the right thing.

Within your own company, you will find the bright, the honest, the hard working, the planners, and those who are willing to learn. As project managers and their managers, you should diligently develop and reward them. You will also find the lazy, the blind optimists, the dishonest, the self-serving, and those who are really not interested in or cut out for the attention to detail necessary in project work. These people must be changed or compensated for with your disciplined and detailed approach until they can be weeded out.

I understand that in our culture, with all of its political correctness and liberal approach to failure, many will object strongly to my thinking and advice. My two mentors, who were major contributors to business and to our national security, were often met with the same response.

If you are one of those who cannot share my assumptions and form of pessimism, hopefully you can accept my process guidance, advice on prime and subcontract administration, and advice on matters like visiting customers and your facilities. I have done my best to touch on all topics I found to be important, but I will say that if you get anything out of this book, take away the principles and processes for planning and the management of variances to your plans, which I discussed in chapter 3.

If you can get past my pessimistic approach and are open to my many bits of advice, consider that you do not have to accept and deal with all of my advice now at once. Use what you can, adding more until you can build your own experience base. The key is to be confident, have fun, and grow until you can rely on that experience base of yours.